THE UNKNOWN AUTHOR
SECOND EDITION

JAMES R. SANER II

The Unknown Author
Copyright © 2014 by James R. Saner II. All rights reserved.

No part of this publication may be reproduced, stored in a retrieval system or transmitted in any way by any means, electronic, mechanical, photocopy, recording or otherwise without the prior permission of the author except as provided by USA copyright law.

Published in the United States of America

ISBN: 9798306221328
1. Poetry / American / General
2. Philosophy / Mind & Body
14.03.13

The Unknown Author

The Unknown Author,
Caught between space & time
He is present in our world,

Who's got a question for our guest tonight?
Is it answerable? Yes, anything you want to know
He's written it down.

The Unknown Author
Is full of love, can predict the future for us all

Do we see him? Yes we do
He is a part of everything,
The Universal God!

Big Star many awards,
He made actors of us all,
Created life with his bright colored pen,
Many books in the collection.

James R. Saner II

For windows are doorways too
Just got to jump through
Take a look inside…

The Music

The Music
Fills your soul
Like the ancient river.
Danger is not
A loud
Entrance
In this most Sacred Place
The circle is around us
Protecting us,
& what you see
Is unheard of

The Voice
You hear remains unseen
Who is it?
I don't know,
The face of mystery
The one who fights
Eternal death

James R. Saner II

The savior of souls laid to rest.
Come
Follow me-
The Music is calling me to walk the narrow road
Not long till this journey has passed
& there you will find your Path
Today is really tomorrow

Free United

Through the woods they traveled to the spot
Bright light hovered through the air,
The most amazing form of energy,
They saw the fire & chose to dance
In a sacred manner
All across the four corners

The Sacred One
The one of peace came &
Danced with them
His name "Wakan Tanka"
If you prefer Holy Spirit,
All the Knowledge of

We called you to become one with
you, Oh Great Universe:
Balance of the Spirit, Mind, & Body.

They were impressed with his brilliance,
The two that came felt unworthy,
Always welcome
Was asked?
YES
Came across the Universe in light speed
The Dance is never ending
Through life the spirits will guide you &
Walk with you throughout all time
One is the Universe
You are no longer a slave but balanced,
Focused, not afraid.

Protected, loved, together we join- FRIENDS
The two men went into the land to share Knowledge
They opened their hearts & shared everything
The only ones that listened were the spirits
OLD-YOUNG
It makes no difference
Everyone is welcomed,
Everyone has their own way,
Welcome to Free United awakening!

The Word Called "Love"

Emotion,
Feeling,
&
Sorrow
Words of Love
No man or woman can deny it
It is a power stronger than everything else
Putting its arms around you &
squeezing the life out of you
Not saying it is a bad thing,
Just an unreliable resource
Feelings for one person may change &
Pass you by,
Some say love is a river
Flowing from day to day
Not leaving any trace that it has been there,
Just a happy feeling for one simple person

James R. Saner II

The one you Love
Sad but true
I've been there

Lines between Us

Between the lines is what you need to see
Between the lines you find certainty
Between the lines truth is reality
Justified in no aspect is the heart's mellow beat
No advantage can you seek
Beyond the lines lives life's frustrations
Split in half are all the Nations
No common ground for peace
Between the lines is where it's at, all in Harmony
Between the lines you have to see
We are all alike- Universal Beings
Right or wrong, it doesn't matter
Between the lines comes after,
It starts with you & it starts with me,
We have to communicate to truly be free
So do your part & I'll do mine
Brotherhood for all Mankind!!!

Dreaming is Sweet

Where do my thoughts end &
Yours begin? All in the same instant
Which point of view can we imagine?
What's real is questioned,
Did we forget that we are still animals?
Nature's Creation,
Energy into Mass
Simple equation
Dreaming is Sweet- Just so happens to be the answer,
Thoughts always moving traveling
beyond, Never concluding
That we are connected.
Same DNA pattern,
Scientific Notation
Which school are we in? The one of education or
The school of Life & its experience?
Who's the bigger man?
Or is he not mentioned
Non-existent

The Unknown Author

How equal are we in the creation?
Sounds pretty different in the long run,
Do we have the same goals?
The same destination?
I would like to go back home,
Back to the beginning- Before we started evolving
Have some peace & quiet
Rest & relaxation
No Measure of time
No need for patience.
What would we gain if that happened?
Probably certain boredom
In other words nothing!
Why this world,
Why is it significant?
The mind seems trapped in its own dimensions
Like a time bomb ready to be detonated or
Like a flower about to blossom
Beautiful in the image shown
Anxious for it to happen
Ready for the Great Awakening
The Mystery of the Unknown

The Unknown Life

Indian Tribes split apart,
Native ways thrown out
The Government wants to educate them,
But the Government really just wants their land.
So beautiful was their home &
So willing to share,

The Governments greed forced them to fight
Made them look like savages come out of the night
All the Indians wanted to do was protect
the most important thing
Known as Life

Why so much hate involved I often wonder,
Why couldn't we relate instead of almost eliminate
Their whole population?

The Grandfathers protected them for awhile
& warned the Indians to stay away from these evil tyrants.

The Unknown Author

The Tribes decided not to stick together,
They broke the circle &
Soon the wars began
Indians traded with these men,
In the end the Government took back their gifts
Out of the Indians' dying hands.

Nature will guide us as it has before
Back to the spirits of our Land
The circle of life is being restored &
I will be a part of this forever,
Still Learning am I but willing to teach
We smoked the pipe in peace.
I am grateful for this life & I thank you
Grandfathers &
The spirits of The Unknown Life

Indian Maiden

Indian Maiden, Bring me your song
Native cities long since gone,
Dance to the Moon, The nights reminisced
Show me your moves, your delicate kiss.
Indian Maiden, come fly with me
Indian Maiden, would you die for me?
The dance is far from done.
Teach you the words, the song will be sung

Spread the joy, our brightest light,
Children will dance day & night
No stopping now, the celebration has come- Join us

Indian Maiden, have you heard- The Voice?
If so, what will be your choice?
To dance around life's fire soaring ever
higher, don't through it aside,
There are no goodbyes

The Unknown Author

I see something beautiful in your eyes, a culture almost lost
But saved by the mind's memory,
The start of something, cause for rebirth,
Children are we wrapped in infancy
Close the door & you gain nothing.

But if left open you gain more than ever imagined,
More than you bargained for
See it, Feel it, Touch it; the spectacle, my friend
Ancient is he the Great one God or Man?
Does it really matter which is he, why not follow or lead-
He is both, you see
Come with the triangle that has four sides,
But only three are visible to the human eyes.

Not far from death are we until life casts its light &
Shadows are made- to hide in.
You must teach me this dance of life & after,
Maiden you are my tool to reach the masters,
Without it there is no song & no
resurrection of times long gone,
Bring them back, my sweet one

Your ancestors call requesting an answer,
Give them one & come
Let's all have some fun, the time to
celebrate is upon us now,

The Walk of Life

Walking down the winding road
listening to stories untold,
Searching for the heart's desire in a
place reflected by a camp's fire,
Circled tents are what appeared
There were six, maybe seven higher than the rest,
Perched but scattered among the trees
in the place three know best.
Why do you come—to find value?
Or is it something else?
What is your question, your uncertainty?
The dawn has left & dusk has crept in
To share its darkness from within. (The Darkened Light)
The Moon gleams on,
Three little birds singing their song
perched among the clouds,
It's where they belong
Different from all the rest,
God has no protest.

The Unknown Author

Their Journey is clear, the light's been turned on,
Not as focused, just follow along
The Ancestors will come beating their drums
War has been declared, it's okay to be scared
Let your heart take rhythm of the drums.
They will protect you from thy enemy's hands & raise you
To victory in the battle not yet won.
So raise your spear & do what needs to be done.
Faith be the key, & through the war cry you will see
The GHOST Dance of the Ancient One

Sparrow

Bless Him
He is the Wiseman, who knows
ALL
But Nothing

On your knees slaves
The Sparrow might be watching,
Mocking the world he sees &
Taking pleasure in your torment.
He wished it this way & for you
To find the day to lie in.
Find the Sun, he is the one,
The divider of night has no End
Only stages guide him,
Speaking of honesty, the path taken
Will lead you home, to dwell in a house
All alone

The Unknown Author

Self-determination, strength in working hard
Steps of conquering no so far
But little by little the Light gets brighter
& you find the journey once again,
To take you away & up someplace caught in a wind
Breeze of life & storms of death slowly go by,
Places you've been cross through the pupil's eye.
Caught in the center, still traveling on,
The Sparrow still singing his song,
Start the dance, get trapped in a trance,
Let your mind go wandering on,
To the Sparrow's house you call home—
Heaven's Nest,
The beginning of life,
The End of death & darkness.

Conversation with Who?

Come to the house upon the Rising Sun,
Which sits waiting for you.
Waiting to be vacant no more,
Waiting for the doors to come open once again.

"Maybe later but not now, a teepee
for me & a hill to sit upon
So my vision quest might be done, would
do just fine for now & forever."

Forever is quite a long time to sit upon the hill,
Don't be like Jack & fall for Mary
who's got those crystal eyes
& ripened cherry,
She is too pure & innocent for your taste.

"Mary is perfect, don't you see, she is
the woman of my dreams.
The one that calls me in my sleep

The Unknown Author

To come & see the destiny that awaits,
In Darkness I will find her light, which
makes the days turn night."

You really think you'll find her, she is gone—Just a myth.
What you need is the house upon the Rising Sun,
Where there is dishes to be cleaned & chores to be done.

"I will serve no one who thinks they are higher than me,
My path leads to righteousness & my goal is to be free
To swim in the skies & fly in the seas
There I will be content & made happy,
So leave me now & do business somewhere later
Peace be upon you, my trusted friend."
To be completed at another time.

"My Friend come, come talk with me,"
My Friend answers with no response,

Go ahead & speak your pleasure,
My right ear is upon you;

"What you said earlier about the house,
Is that the same house which lit me on fire &
showed me the dance of the cool moon?
You know the place where all the nations are one"

James R. Saner II

I know of no place united & free,
My place though is someplace far
from here, someplace special
Delicate to the human eyes
Something you have already seen.

"Why not the heart,
That is where the soul is,
For without sight I still see, for my Angels gifted me
They laid their hands on me with the
most delicate of touches".

What was the Gift?
"Something Incredible?"

I will give you life under roof upon
the house of the Rising Son,
What more do you need?

"I need to fly like the Crow & swim
with the Dolphin as the Whale,
For that is what I am & that is what I must be.
That place is coming, it's coming upon
two now— a certain peace."

You speak of peace, do you actually believe it?
It's dead to the world, dead to the soul.

The Unknown Author

What you say can't ever be, that path leads to insanity.

"I say to you of disbelief, I am sane as any, but maybe
To be insane would the sanest of all,
Do you believe in the living dead?"

Is it the living dead or the dead living that you speak of?
You are but a child who knows nothing of
the real world in which you exist.
But I, I am far beyond your world—
For I live in a world of my own, the
world of infinite many!

"What makes you greater than he who
walks peacefully upon mother Earth?
I say there is no one greater than the peace maker,
Or you might know him better as the Creator of all.
That is where my loyalty belongs."

If I were he & he were me, then would you come & go
With divinity to the place I know best, some say its West,
Others though they love the cold &
will also go to the North
To seek my presence. But I am all around

The Ying & The Yang
All in one—One among many.

James R. Saner II

You have proven yourself worthy,
This conversation is done!

"Then I will go with peace
Among friends in the circle of life."

The Bailo De Deus

Vio qunn Deus—
The love of a nation,
Faith of Deus comes from the hearts of men.
Freedom to be one— Once again the circles complete
With me joined together in the Bailo De Deus!
The beat keeps on beating
The circle of life is forever rotating
Counter clockwise,
Ancient mystery.

Life in Deus many dreams,
Deus forever living.
We are all the creation with the
chapters moving—NO STOP!
Because it's the experience written.

History in the making we are—
Forever present in the writing,

James R. Saner II

Deus is many, Mankind is awaking
from a long magical sleep.
Let's start learning & remembering what we are,
Truly created,
In Deus you see.
Love the name & love the creation,
It's time for Thanksgiving
Vio qunn Deus,
Always in eternity,
Go with God
Peace, Love, & Harmony

The Watcher

The killer is watching me, I do believe
stalking eyes can't stay,
The game hasn't been played
The end is faraway.
It's only begun so leave the curtains drawn,
The performer is about to take stage.
Stay as a dream for as long as you can,
But leave the door swung open,
Let me see what is about to come,
If you wish I will pray unspoken.
Don't leave me hanging in suspense,
The scene is too intense, waiting just can't be done
Do I have say in all that's become?
Or just a puppet am I hung on a string
Not choosing my fate, my own destiny
That can't be the case,
I want my own place upon the minds of memory.
I will not be rubbed out like the native one,
You smoked his pipe in peace, then stole it from them,

You are the evil that lies within,
polluting the heart with sin.
Cast you aside we did, but the time has come,
& come again it did & soon it will be done.
Your voyage will be over
The war will be won
Days of light have appeared
Nights of fright are gone,
Cosmic Energy remains constant…

The Tree

The Tree,
The Tree,
How it seems to be happy
I sit under
That tree with
Its fallen leaves
All around me.
The Breeze is Light
& sings a song
Of an ancient land.
I never want to leave my tree again,
So peaceful is my tree,
He lets me climb his branches,
Perched like a bird enchanted.
The smell is fresh
& with it I am blessed
A feeling of nature is planted!
The Tree,
The Tree,

James R. Saner II

The top seems to be too high,
It's like climbing a mountain,
But not hopeless is this matter,
For one day I will build a ladder.

But for now I am content on sitting under my tree
With a wish I can try later.

Carry Man

Carry Man, Carry Man, Carry me away,
Carry Man, Carry Man, I don't want to stay
Take me now—AWAY
To your house we'll play
Do you know what love is, Mr. Carry Man?
Can you share some with me—I don't want
to be a bad man, Mr. Carry Man—
Only want to be a Shaman Man.
Helpful hints, no mean tricks—just there.
Carry Man, Carry Man, Come visit me,
Cary Man, Carry Man, just to be free.
I know what peace is, let me tell you.
How can I make this world better now?
Or is it in my hands?
Carry Man, Carry Man, I thank you for being a friend,
Anytime you want to go, always ready to leave…

Dog Tale

A boy & his dog, what a sight
One without the other just wouldn't be right.
Alone no more,
My new best friend is laying on the floor,
With his protective eyes fixed on me
As I turn my head to sleep.
The night turns to day at the blink of an eye.
Awakened by a lick, that seems really sick,
But it's something I look forward to,
For the rest of my adolescent days.

She was a good dog, who would soon have pups
To take her place, but I just couldn't let that be the case
So when they arrived, Dad & I took a drive to the vet,
Who would care for the pups till they each found a home
In a young person's life.

The Second

Beautiful,
But not first,
The Second.
Come gather round,
Everyone in this town is invited.
Choices in life come gather around Christ,
You're always welcome.
No lies,
Peace in the heart
It's a new start
It's a tough one—(not really)
The Second.
Look who's around,
You'll lose your frown
The Second.
It's something you'll have to share or
Beware of the down that's possible to happen.
Christ
Lord & Master,

Friend who's always there for you & I together
The Second.
Not afraid of dying when he is around,
I feel respected.
Doesn't matter what anybody says
As long as he's there protecting.
Even when you are alone & feeling
like something's missing,
He's always there, just have to find him
The Second.
Your choice that was given in the beginning of time
Respect him.
Love is a hard thing to do, (Not so much)
Cherish it
The Second.
II

Graduation Day

Graduation day,
Time to just kick back & say thank you, my friend
You were with me till the end.
Life has opened a door & I will follow your lead—
Enter into the unknown world of tomorrow.
For eternity has called my number,
No time for slumber or delay,
Life just fades away,
It is time to catch the bus
As it pulls off the curb,
My ticket is already bought,
Don't get choked up.
Staying cool & staying calm
I enter in the chase & catch the bus
Then win my race
For destiny knows its place on
Graduation Day.

The Church I Speak of

The Church I speak of
Is something like this, its walls are
spread out with no bricks.
Its foundation solid ground.
The most Holy place with the most perfect view.
The sky is the roof, the highest steeple
What better place to hold communion.
The perfect setting with Nature
spreading as far as you can see
Believe me it's beautiful.
It's all around.
The Church I speak of
Has its own rules
You have to be living in order to come.
I do believe that includes me as well as you.
So let us live in peace & come together to worship.
Friends of Nature,
Nature is all—it's what we are,
No need for confusion.

Care but Don't

Selfless caring for you or not at all for them.
Someone said them,
Yet I said us in us.
Caring for you & you alone
Is a heartless task
Lonely as well as empty.
Care for those who share with you the
knowledge of life & love—
The underestimated emotion.
Happy as you want to be,
In your heart you will always be free.
Do not turn down help at any time,
For the lender will one day be the
one who needs something.
Who better than you
To be the difference in kindness,
Care but don't care,
In the sense what people think of you
Remember not to judge life or

James R. Saner II

Others that aren't like you,
Share the Love.
No appetite for sour bread,
Be strong in Spirit as it guides you
through life's long struggle,
Always thanks!
Thank you for the Earth & its species,
But more thanks in breathing.
Never turned away,
Always focused Always!

American Dream

Life is worth living when it comes from a dream,
Today is a new day which yesterday shadowed.
You take in everything taught, so you might one
day take it out among the world & teach it.
The American Dream is one of Freedom
Some might share it, others will keep it to themselves,
With little fulfillment or maybe even none at all.
But for me the gift of giving seems by far the best choice,
So it has worked out well.
I find that it's my destiny to be The Poet,
One who shares from the heart.
The giver with the gift that keeps on giving
Who gives till death to help people out.
With a feast of friends long since seen,
Waiting beyond the gates of the golden city.
The books been written & only a few
have been chosen to read,
As for me I am one among these chosen,
I have been blessed with a story to tell.

James R. Saner II

The Story is not false or fiction,
But simple truths laid upon the heart.
The goal of mine & a few others is to
open the eyes of all the rest,
So they can see the soul that God has blessed.
That is my goal The American Dream,
To share what has been given to me.
Some think it's crazy & that's OK,
Others bow their heads to pray.
I want to hear their wants & needs,
Just to help out spiritually.
So much to do with so little time,
But through the eyes of a Poet time is of no importance.
People will hear what I have to say,
Maybe not now but someday.
Many souls will be reborn & the Creator will be praised.
That my friend is The American Dream.

The day of the Poet will come,
When his life on Earth is done
& no one will forget to thank him for the works he gave.
There will be many tears on this dark snowy day,
But not of sorrow—no way
For he has been set free,
By the accomplishment of his American Dream.
It is fun to think about, but hard to do,

The Unknown Author

With the help of others it might someday come true,
You can bet on it—
Anyone?

Always

I will love you, Always
Always thinking of you, Always
One & one makes two, Always
But really it isn't true, Always
Should be united, Always
Instead of divided, Always
Always right there, voice riding on air
Always! Always! Always!

Soldiers

The Unknown Soldier
Who was lost at war,
No one knew him, no one cared.
Just let him lie there on the ground
Not even one frowned at the sight
Of his tattered body.
One man later said make a grave,
Yeah—make a grave for Unknown Soldiers
Make a grave for the boys
Who lost everything & gained nothing on our behalf,
Then vanished from our thoughts.
We owed them our thanks,
Yet never gave it.
What is left to do?
Dig the hole & fill it with the Unknown Soldier
Or take him home & let him stay,
Where he can rest in peace
With friends whose names are missing.
Another said later on that war is a tragic thing,

James R. Saner II

But I say the war is not tragic
As long as you make
The Unknown
Known & let them have eternal rest…

Not just about them

A child's spirit always wants to find out.
A child's spirit fresh & new—
Sounds good to me,
How about you?
We can learn a lot from our children,
Love never ending.
They are not afraid of sharing with others who are caring,
They are the gift of Joy whose emotions are overflowing.
When I see a child I can't help but smile,
So important is a new life.
We are the ones that show the way, &
With each new day they grow & play.
Join the children in their game &
You will receive unearned praise,
Because to a child they see you care not just about them,
But about everything.
They can see inside you & bring out that
child who's grown up & forgotten.
Be observant with your child

James R. Saner II

Let the spirit connect &
Joy you have met
Imagination you thought you had forgotten.
Show them Freedom &
Show them respect,
Because they are not dumb,
But bright with full intellect.
If I could be a child again,
I would want to try everything I hadn't
& I know I can because a child grown
up is still a child at heart,
That's what makes this life more
Special & Fun
So care for your child
& show them your spirit
Play with them,
Nothing should be more
Important than the children.

Day turns Night

Sky beams,
High beams,
Highway passing
The day turns night
As the sun sets over the horizon.
Winding, dining
Your date slips & her hand lands in your lap.
Eyes as clear as crystal waters,
Even more white sands coat the inside lining of the mind.
Nature be my maiden,
Protect her I'm saying,
The unfit Humans who took
Her grace & beauty.
You will be my request
I ask then receive, No Bullshit
Love your neighbor &
Love your friends

James R. Saner II

Peace till the Ends
Make time start all over & begin again.
(That's Romance Baby, want some?)

Infinity

Let me show you infinity as we now speak—
What it means to be free
Never ending
~Sleep~
A dream we never awake
Infinite ways
Spirits pretending to be lost
In a world that is fake—manmade.
There is no final chapter in this book,
The writer maintains & is happy,
Each word has meaning & opens a door to creativity.
Do we see it as it is happening?
Maybe,
You & I are a part of this book
As is always everything.
Big or small
Fat or skinny,
All in the way you perceive it
Joy in living,

James R. Saner II

Have you not yet met the soul you seek?
Well, it's right here in this
Thought for Today
The chance we have to take,
Fear is Hate,
But Love is creating
Pride & spirit from day to day.
Just like the writer as characters we maintain.
Does it get better?
Is a question that is asked
But as the character you are free in your role.
Experience everything you wished to create,
You might call it heavenly,
But some call it Awake.
The Great Awakening of our cultures
There is no end to the beginning
No door not already open
You choose which way you take.

I choose to seek knowledge of
Everything & to love creating.
We are all a bunch of nothing
But infinity is the same,
Freedom by God's Law
No law at all, JUST FAITH
The heart is great & if you choose to dance with the spirit
You dance as equals,

The Unknown Author

Beings of the race.
No death in this game, no darkness from within,
Just fun & infinite.
Infinity goes on & on,
Just see it's there
Never leaves you—
You have been found for many years
Whatever that means…

"This is the End" of my pen

What is the end?
That start of a new beginning.
A friend indeed the end, the friendship that never ends.
You find most peace beyond fear but
fear is a treacherous thing
To enter into. You don't know what lies beyond,
But we do
We of the three that form a sign,
The sign of all man.
Passed fear is the greatest of peace, your being—
Your friend the end
There is the doorway so open the door
& exit into the other side.
Where the end has no end & windows
of the mind are shattered,
But stand in place of all time.
Look out & see the eyes that are watching,
They're watching you as well as me, calling eyes,
Calling eyes, that truly see

The Unknown Author

Borrow those eyes & bring them into spread their light &
Show you the most incredible life
The Movie—
What a film it is.
I have seen it time & time again.
Can't miss the next show,
Be seated
Let your mind go (Traveling)

Give & Be the Giver

Your hearts justice never went to trial
Blocking communication with denial.
On whose head does the blame fall?
On mine I guess,
But I still protest just time to move on.
Out of my hands I had to find out
The possibilities of this
One sunned world
Who comes to worship?
I do now
Always did, just didn't understand it yet.
It is coming as love & understanding
In space & time
Can you receive it?
All the warmth & wetness—Paradise
Imagine the possibilities of sharing & not caring
What you get in return,
Give & be the Giver in talk
&

The Unknown Author

Communication
Lend your knowledge
Jump on the fantasy cruise with all the colored light,
Love & Dreams, then come true tonight.
Sea of wisdom—Light—
Paradise is yours to create,
Just need to get creative.
Listen to the children &
Follow their innocence so you are not lost as well
Everyone's invited,
Can you make it?
Did you like it?
Are you back home comforted by blankets?
Were you scared or just excited?
Or is there even anything there but normal
Everyday life?
I think it's something more—
& I like it

I know of a Few

My whole life
Has been here in the wheat fields of Kansas
Time for a change,
A new home town!
Arizona Deserts, Indian campgrounds?
Islands Paradise?
Purpose to be found,
Wisdom to be shared,
To the growing population who really do care.
New communications,
Old ways of insight.
Here comes the millennium
~Age of Enlightenment~
The new light
Who wants to be found?
I know of a few,
We are small in number

The Unknown Author

But big in heart,
Warriors for life,
Warriors for you!

Children of the Son

Burning Star
How long has it been?
Night seemed like it would never end.
Hope from a distance over the horizon.
Children of the Sun come again,
Something always happens when
Day starts & Night ends.
Magic—how the Earth spins.
One direction balanced in space,
Pretty amazing thing as it happens.
Children of the Sun, dance &
Sing songs of awakening.
Dream your dream at the beginning of dawn,
Awake from your sleep,
Children of the Son.
Burning Star lifetimes old,
Pleased to meet you, your story's being told.
The warmth is felt throughout the Universe
One small planet given birth,

The Unknown Author

Children of the Sun, Burning Star you named.
We choose to worship the creation & it's Creator.
We call it the sun because it's bright,
Every ray gives off new life.
We of the Sun are one small candle,
Who will be the first to see our bright lantern?
& Come visit before it turns night
Children of the Son, Lovers of beauty,
What better way to live truly?

The is of Now

The is of Now,
God is the is
Which is a constant of how,
Answer is common ground.
Acceptance of the lead,
Imagine more depth than what you see—
Peace
Lingering
Within
ME

Told once

*If anyone in the class
Was asked that question
They all would be able to give the right answer.
Everybody knows the correct answer to that question.*
A friend told me once that I was the Devil
I asked him then where is my Hell?
All around is society &
Things that cause chaos &
Are very confusing.
This Earth is no Hell,
But could be if you make it the way they say it should be,
Do not bow, just stand and see the Great
Spirit swaying in the trees.
Do you see the sun which gives off light &
Allows your eyes to see?
Did you awake & realize it was only a dream?
A myth what some say is fantasy,
The realm of creativity
Signs of the time, just common scare,

James R. Saner II

The unknown mystery that captures people everywhere.
One day maybe everyone will have open eyes &
Be able to realize the spirit inside.
The infinite being never ending
She has many labels:
God, Spirit, Angel, Man, Serpent
Indeed all about everything,
No good or evil where I stand.
All about life in this hidden land of Americans

The Auction

Girls are swarming in the hotel,
The feast was being set up,
I hear soft conversations from a distance,
As
I serve the Host for tonight's presentation.
So low,
So low,
My tickets free,
I can't imagine paying.
Not because of money even though I have none.
I couldn't afford it anyway,
That is why I'm serving the drinks.
Tonight's presentation will bring you great joy
Too bad the people who need it weren't invited.
So I guess you don't need it after all
It is something we all own,
It's called a soul
Only the rich were allowed entrance into the Auction.

The White Life

Look up there,
The stars are gone
The sky is cloudy,
Snow is falling all around.
The Earth is warm & hibernated
The city slow in moving,
Too quick in thought to grasp the
White crystal beauty
The cycle of time
The rotation of season
How long has it been?
I can't imagine
Lifetimes fall,
Like the white in the skies
Covering the Earth's surface
Hill to Mountain
Such joy is unnoticed,
The Mothers taken for granted
Nature forgotten

The Unknown Author

All you see is yourself trapped with
others on some lonely planet,
What about the animals who have no place to go?
Because they are too scared to confront us.
We are the mighty men with great inventions,
Too lazy to care for our surroundings.

To the Snow I speak
In a humble sacred manner,
My friend,
I thank you for your time
& Goodness
Stay with us,
We can build a white snowman
Or
Go through the deserted forest many years been planted
I can just imagine Snow Heaven
Angels made in the Snow,
Frost on all the windows & houses.
Society frozen
As it stands.
I love your cool warmth of Magic,
Can you see the people's prison?
Let us free them from dull captivity &
Show them Freedom in our holy white presence
Winter began in an instant...

No Ordinary Show

*The motors running,
The performers jump in.
"Good show I take it?"
Yes Dynamic*

The stage was dark with colored lights flashing
Crowds swarmed & started slashing,
At the edge of the city
Big bodies were holding
Protecting the stars as they go on,
Ready to dance & sing their songs
Of ancient wonders.
It was no ordinary show
The energy in the auditorium was Cosmic.
The drums started beating &
The audience grew silent

The low voice called out, "Are you Ready?"
"Let's start the madness for this evening!"

The Unknown Author

Soon the roar engulfed the speaker &
The women started throwing their panties.

"All right, we got some naked ladies tonight!"
"Would you like to hear some poetry?
Well that's good because we got some"
"The city in the night,
Surrounded by artificial light,
Who blew out the light?
We want to know!!!
Very good, pretty creative—
Now you can see the stars in Nature's Creation.
Love the heavenly ocean.
We can swim &
Fly constant for many lifetimes."

How did we get back in the limo?

One of the performers was disoriented.
"Good show I take it?"
Yes Dynamic

Take us home,
But first let's go get some coffee
Cup of Java sounds pretty tasty.
Time slipped for an eternal moment.

The Lord of the Radio

The Lord of the Radio
Changes the station,
Gets sick &
Tired of all the pointless information
He wants to hear music
Words to a song,
To sing along with it as he's driving along,
Nowhere destinations,
Has nowhere to go,
It doesn't matter because he is Lord of the Radio.
He likes to travel
With the volume up loud.
Can't stand to be interrupted by radio announcers.
If guests are present in the passenger's seat,
He makes his own tune with
A magical beat,
All the way through the commercial interruption
Until the radio roars with
Poetic Justice

The Unknown Author

He is the man driving the car
The Lord of the Radio,
The ruler of Rock,
He is lonely in an empty car…

Perfect We Are

What did you do to deserve such torture?
Nothing can be recalled,
Only searching for who you are—is answered.
God help me, please
I beg of thee, do not forsake me.
I am all alone & I'm in trouble,
Spirit of the unknown, come back home
Fill my heart with warmth & love
Guide me in this messed up world
What is really, won't be tomorrow.
I have found a woman so beautiful,
She is a princess (My Queen)
Her name means Sunshine (Kira)
My voice rides on the wind &
Drifts to and from,
What more can I give that you don't already own?
Why is Satan so real to people?
Why was God a fool for letting
someone go with such power?

The Unknown Author

That is downgrading our Heavenly Father,
He doesn't make mistakes.
He just creates who we are
Is he not the end to the beginning?
That means Perfect We Are
Is not everything around us a part of who we are?
Is it not God?
Loving & Caring
Individual Beings still connected in the circle of the tree,
Let us grow &
Be free of all the laws.
Just a man filled with emotion,
Just a father letting go,
But it never happens—
Am I Spirit
Or Am I Man?
The tough part is being both.
I know what I must do,
Travel to the wilderness & get lost,
My vision will come &
I will finally be happy &
Filled with the task of creating.

Ravens

Always a bird man,
Never a word man
Up among the clouds is my haven
For like the Raven—I Am
I find certainty & peace inside.
The doors remain open for those refugees
Who need Shelter
Like a nurtured child
They are let in,
Within they find peace
Through the hidden doorway a
Haze of serenity.
Perched among the walls
As a United One.
Men of the birds fly together & speak softly
Words fly through the night & intervene with the wind
Together silent voices are heard through the air,
Warning of troubles,
Speaking of Past,

The Unknown Author

Ravens
A very dear friend wrote this one with me.
Thanks to Jeremy M. Buckallew

What I said earlier

What I said earlier,
For my ears only, I guess.
I have heard many protests
About what I bring to the table.
It's your choice, my opinion
Just go with what life brings you.
I was just trying to help,
For God the universal being
Has come to me
In more than just a dream.
I know what is false
I see things differently &
More clear than you can possibly imagine.
I want to show the world
What it is like to see with childlike eyes,
Always something new to think about.
Jesus was the same way,
He was the son of God & a brother of mine.
He was no different from you or me

The Unknown Author

You can talk to God, too.
Make things happen in time of need,
All you need is faith,
Faith in what you believe.
It only takes one small mustard seed.
It's true—shows all through History
What good is information if you can't share it?
Just not time yet, I guess.

The Brotherhood

Let's fight for the cause,
Life makes warriors of us all
Do the duty with no pause,
Join the Brotherhood
It calls & calls for the mighty braves.
Women & children are protected in the invisible city
Laying under the fog.
So stay a little while longer,
Then you will praise the names of the lost,
Every battle fought
Every battle won.
Love the rage &
Learn to handle it kindly.
Young man you have heart,
Let it guide you.
The eyes of the Past—Present—Future
Gods are always watching
Take notice, don't be afraid
They request your presence on this fine day.

The Unknown Author

We are the front line survivors of this war
Our weapons are swords.
Let us prepare for battle
Come feast with us, you of the new.
Forget about the Devil, he is dead!!!
Our enemies look too much like Humans.
This war of course is imaginary, for
the spirit's pleasure alone,
Does it matter? Of course it's who we are.
But one day we will die in bloodshed to spread
A new message of life &
Forever change the course of History.
Sounds pretty impressive to be an Indian brave,
We fight in faith for something we believe.
All life is important always,
Will there ever be a change in living?
Death has many faces,
Death makes Angels of us all.
Enter the night & come with us
Over to the other side of God,
The pure one—Peace
I love Freedom all names be praised,
They are the same
Equal

Fires are lit

Don't be there,
You can't remember where
Your hat is hung
Go downstairs
It all starts there on your journey home.
Fires are lit,
It's time to split
Out of here I come.
Doors opened wide
Out we fly
Midnight still too young.
Don't go yet
We need to sweat
Sauna, here we come
Pants pulled up
Shirt untucked
To the river we run.

The Unknown Author

Water haven
Where is my maiden?
Bring her I call
Silence was the only response.

Dog War

What transpired out of the dog war
Was sweet & cool
It seemed to touch the young son's human eyes,
Made them glow, made them thankful to be alive.
Spirit of the dog gave us reason to call on God,
Or maybe it was just time too
Populations limited
Some no longer willing to survive,
So they called upon death only to
realize they were still alive
In their own broken down reality stuck in time,
Freedom will surely shine,
Like the stars in the Heaven
No laws, No limits, No death.
Just great existence in the circle of life.
Do you think God will crucify you
for not obeying the Bible?
Only if that is what you wish,
Because you feel you are inferior—lower than slime.

The Unknown Author

I did & came to realize that this journey
is for all time—never ending.
It is life the gift of creating,
Using your imagination,
Finding your soul a part of everything
far greater than your body.
Did you experience who you are?
Not who you were because you still are.
Now remembering other lives from
long ago is a different matter,
Your soul just grows & grows
Gets bigger & continues on through space & time.
I love you is to be considered—GOD

Hibernation

So here I am
Back in the hot seat again
I feel no different,
But still I am not the same.
Fighting with struggles
Unaffected by
Everything in life taken for granted
As age just flies by.
Will I be OK?
I think so,
I am a mouse caught in a maze,
Everyone wants to share their opinions
But can't stand to hear mine in return.
I am tired of fighting
So I take a new approach,
Just go with it &
Be even quieter
Still in hibernation.
I take the bear's approach

The Unknown Author

Ready for action,
Ready to mark territorial boundaries.
But not until I am out of this place of slavery,
A place where there is no peace,
No one wanting to get along,
Even worse no common ground.
I wish these people would listen to me,
They think they know God,
Even better that I don't.
Where they came up with that
I don't know.
I give up everything I have & am
To the Great Spirits that be.
Just a piece of the puzzle trying to find my place
All throughout History.
But first I have to find me,
In order to achieve the Freedom it brings.
It's tough but it's coming along
Ready for my heavenly home.
Ready for the reason I am here &
The people I'm supposed to help.
Whoever they be
I'm willing…

Time Unmeasured

Traveling beyond the atmosphere
At a speed of time unmeasured,
Light—Bright covering everything in its sight
Still the same as time unmeasured,
Everything always greater.
Pure energy constant stream
Covered like an ocean
Or a field of grain
Big Gigantic Monster.
Did you see that thing?
What was it, Imaginary?
Real or just me?
The beach,
Sand in an individual's hands
Slowly passing through our fingers.
Hold it for a moment &
See how it feels
Love it.
This land is surely magnificent,

The Unknown Author

Space age can't handle it.
What's the scientific notation?
Can you let it go &
Live with it?
You just want the experience
Truth is impressive,
Energy that connects me to the other dimensions
Free my Old & Sacred Spirit
Everyone's eyes are welcome,
No fear of opinion,
None is unimportant.
Let us travel forever,
Together,
Come here
Over there,
Missed it.
Nope you've got it,
Almost forgot it,
Didn't you?
Or was that just part of the experience?
Congratulations,
You've graduated.
Time to live in full satisfaction.
Safe & forever
Warm & happy.
Share the Message.

Ocean of Death

Nations
Rise
By the *tides of blood*
An Ocean of Death surpasses.
People used to conquer
Then forgotten when the wars are through.
Misused power,
It only lies in the hands of a few.
No one fights for Freedom
Only for money.
Friendships abused
&
Wasted.
The people are dying
The governments are still crying—more
I have nothing against you.
Until you kill the innocent.
You'd better watch out.
The people are calling

The Unknown Author

For another revolution.
Honestly what is it you're trying to prove?
Maybe I can listen.

Prophet/ Saint

These messages that we write
For thoughts of a new & better life
Are fading.
Anymore all you find is chaos,
No more dreams accomplished.
Your success has dropped to an all-time low.
The Savior has forgotten your soul,
Now who will lead you?
We don't need one king—but many with the hearts of life.
If you want to live, you better start moving
& Talk to your Christ or Creator,
Get his ass back here so we all don't burn
Like last night's dinner.
Call me a new aged prophet or an old Bible saint
All I'm saying is this world is crashing.
I still see the good in things, the beauty of the creation.
Yet the people are pushing for destruction & money,
The power struggle is amazing.
So pray or meditate for simple human awareness

The Unknown Author

Or solution to these problems.
The Movie "Armageddon" was right,
The Human species has the capability
to maintain its life for centuries,
On the downside we could destroy it tomorrow.
Simple Truth,
I wish it were more,
I might not have the power of the universe in my hands
Or the wisdom of Christ & his followers.
But I seem to have more,
My Freedom
The gift of falling on your face or making a mistake,
Being able to stand up & understand the lesson
For each & every day.
You & I both are capable of achieving.
Reach for the stars & you will find they aren't out of reach
Not too far.
Have patience,
My Friends,
My fellow members of this community.

Move On

My Voice,
Lost
Taken by greed.
All I can do is
Write & Read.
Mainline communications
The networks shut down,
My voice is
Body language,
The Bird
I'm sure you heard that one.
There is no sound coming out of my mouth.
It's there but somebody put the mute button on.
I see you,
I hear you,
But I can't respond to you.
Whoopee Fucking Doo-Dah!
We both need to
MOVE ON

The Death of a Fellow Stranger

The Death of a Fellow Stanger,
We are all sinners who deny forgiveness.
Rebels of Heaven,
Questioners of Hell.
Jesus,
Devils,
Right,
Wrong,
The stranger's journey led them home.
Invisible entities,
Higher vibrations
Freed by our prisons
Trapped by our desires.
The next customer still waits in line,
No choice in that decision,
How may I help you?
The words came before Next or a Number.
This person is really on the ball,
They must care about their job.

James R. Saner II

A volunteer worker
Who cares—too much.
Was willing to die for you
They did,
Their gone.

Water

Quick
On
The draw,
You know who made it all
Damn ghosts are
Haunting this corridor.
How do we get past them?
Do you fight fire with fire?
Instead
Flood it
With the liquid form of water.
Unsalted is preferred,
Salted burns & stings
Cleanses the wound.
Allows it to heal,
Faster.

Escape

Food,
Drink,
Everlasting Dream,
The Nourishment.
Church,
Faith,
Just another *Escape*,
People blinded by Belief.
Movies,
Theaters,
Imagination on screen.
The next one is based
On real life events,
Not as fiction.
Music,
Radio,
Too political,
I miss the *Old Ways!*

Tithe

Common Scare,
Mean people everywhere.
Greedy hands
& Lustful desires
The Pope asks
You for your tithe.
If you don't pay your 10%
You will burn in Hell or
Get stuck in limbo.
The Church is upside down
& Is Backwards.
Why bother
With this pointless Ethic.
You have more
Important things to do,
Your objective is to find
Heaven.

The Death

The Death of a King
The Death of a Queen
The Death of a Religious Leader
The Death of a Child
The Death of an Old Wise Man
The Death of a Family Member
The Death of a Warrior
The Death of a Nation
The Death of Life
The Death of Death
A Stopping point.
Where the story was finished
A new book began,
No rhyme or reason
For its expansion.
Death in a Dream
That is where the world ends
The life of Eternity begins.

It's All Right

It's all right,
You feel depressed
You're over excited,
Unable to comprehend
Your life's struggles.

It's all right
To wish for the end
Or take the time to complete it.
It's your stubbornness that drives you.

It's all right
To question your life's progress
Or make drastic decisions.

It's all right
To be scared
Or confused,
Just don't make a habit of it.

James R. Saner II

It's all right
To long for another
Or request time alone,
#1 priority is you!

It's all right
To have friends
Enjoy your life,
Find out what's bothering you.

It's all right
To make requests
Or even expect things to happen
The way you want them to.

It's all right
No matter what mood.
Or setting.

It's all right
What I'm saying is something's looking after you.
Otherwise you wouldn't be here receiving my message.

It's all right
I hope these words comfort you.

The Unknown Author

Take the time,
Find your purpose.

It's all right
Whatever happens.

Revelation

Ending,
Bending,
Milking relationship,
Like a leach attached to
My energy field,
She nurses my protection,
Moving on,
Now she's gone,
Hopefully she will find what
She's looking for.
The best,
The Worst,
Whichever works,
Who am I to judge you?
The Dream,
The scheme,
My awaking conscious has arrived.
Forests of this world
Explored then destroyed by man.

The Unknown Author

Nature will stop us.
The computer chip above your eyes or
In your arm will haunt you.
Choose death before the warlock comes to find you.
Freedom in a book
It's happening.
The Revelation.

Go & Dream

I want you to go & dream tonight,
I want you to see your life.
Ask in your sleep to hear the secrets,
Ask for remembrance.

I want you to go & dream tonight,
I want you to ask them why,
Make some new friends in the subconscious.

I want you to go & dream tonight,
I want you to receive their power.
They tell me to write these words to you:
Come on in, you are always welcome.

I want you to go & dream tonight,
I want you to meet **Freedom**!

The Unknown Author

I want you to go & dream tonight,
I want you to awake with joyous tear filled eyes.

I want you to go & dream tonight,
I want you to believe in something...

Bondage

Am I blessed or cursed?
With a stroke of my pen
I can get your brain moving.
Trapped is the thought of creativity,
People teach our children
To lock it away & walk away from
Their emotional feelings.
No true growth is allowed to occur.
I can't tell you I'm right,
I know for a fact—
I can't tell you I'm wrong.
There is too much out there
Around us going on,
Yet everyone is brainwashed by a controlled power.
Too naïve maybe to actually see
The conquest that goes on in everyday reality.
Free yourself from bondage
Use the Will that was given to you,
Change the world,

The Unknown Author

Save yourself
& Save the others.
The people are depending on you!

Possession

Possession,
The man didn't understand
When he was asked to sell his possessions.
No wonder moving is such a hassle,
Everyone is tied down to
Commitment & possession.
It's mine
OK
Have it!
Naked I came,
Naked I'm going.
My Death awaits me,
I await My Death.
Humbling moment of Kindness.
Chastised—Imprisoned
Searching for the key,
Who has it?
I asked everyone I ran into
"Pardon me, do you know the answers?"

The Unknown Author

The answer I found was,
No one had a clue
As to what I was looking for.
My Journey I suppose—my questions.
I have the answers,
But do I have the courage to share them?
I'm sharing…

Help Me

Like an Angel
She read my palm
Unlocking all my secrets & charm.
The test of a wondering souls,
The quest for knowledge & wisdom.
God, you are out there I know,
I do believe.

She wasn't afraid to look deep inside me—my soul.
What kind of sign is this?
Is it possible? Yes
California,
Should I go?
I need too!
For how long?
How do I depart?

It's not that easy for an inmate to leave
his prison 18 years being in,

The Unknown Author

I will always survive no question of that,
I just hope I'm not alone.
Either or I'm going.
Asking kindly for guidance,
Please help me,
Help me in my task,
Help me walk my journey,
Help me arrive at my new destination,
a soul that's searching.
Help me to say goodbye, so long for now...

Cookies

Taking
Making
Baking
Some Cookies,

Giving
Sharing
Borrowing
Some Cookies,

Salads
Appetizers
Main Courses
Dessert
The cookies were gone before they were served!

The Unknown Author

I
Have
Nothing else to

Say
For the moment.

I will
Let you
Know
When
It's Time!

It's Time

It's Time
To believe in dreams!
It's Time
For opportunity
To become known &
Share my positive energy with others.
It's Time
To take the Re
Off of Remodeling &
Look to a new city & Destiny.
You like my eyes
My structure needs some work though,
I'm trusting you &
My own decisions,
Like I said
I'm letting coincidence &
Faith lead me to achieve
A once in a lifetime goal.
I'm going to become a model,

The Unknown Author

I'm going to New York.
I'm going to wake up now
Get rich,
Become a Big Star!

Share the Message

Who brings peace that's not already there?
How do you find it?
Just have to be aware—
Of everything!

My view on church is something like this,
People are too afraid of going to hell
They put themselves up & look down.
The question is this,
Where would you be without the Book?
Where would you be if Christ never came down?
But nobody ever asks that question.
It's not relevant, but is that how it really is?

It states in the Bible that you should
share the message of Christ.
It also says in doing so you open that
culture up to the question
Heaven or Hell?

The Unknown Author

Meaning that if they say I believe in
the way that was before me
& before my father,
Then they are going down!
That can't be God,
That part is Man!
The parts that are important are what count—
Peace, Love, & Harmony.

Who makes the wise man & labels him that way?
Only a Man.
So this is how I see things—
You have many choices in life,
You can do well for others in doing
so you do well for yourself.
Religion is not a bad thing, don't get me wrong,
But let us talk about open minds &
the gift to let them out!

Spirit of the unknown seems impossible
But let's find out
What it is we are & how.
Let us forget who is right or wrong.
Let us join hands & dance around in a circle called life.
The tree is at the center with branches spread out.

James R. Saner II

It seems to me impossible,
I insist we find out.
What are you afraid of?
Do you think I am Evil?
I am not.
I am peaceful & full of Love,
Which is what all writings define as God!

If I am willing,
Then I ask you as well,
Will you drop that guard & become still?
Children in the eyes of the spirit—Good
Free will & happiness you have found.

Within you is he,
The wilderness & the sea
All things you can't measure,
But something you see & know of as Nature.
That was the beginning,
Do you think you are favored?
That is not what it's about.
Mature in thinking, let's work it out.

All little things in everyday life show you,
But you don't think they do or they just don't count.
So now I say
Who will be the bigger person & lower their hands

The Unknown Author

& accept the offer, it still stands.

Respect on both parts,
Equals in being,
If we all join together
Then the world starts living.

But not everyone will agree,
They are too scared to find out,
With that I pause
With a feeling I now know as peace.

God's Presence

What is it?
Invisible, Unbelievable, Powerful
Can't imagine living without it.
Love come with us
Share us in this time of need,
Special moment
Time captivating,
Questions asked, then answered.
God Free
Full of Spirit—Happy!
No more hunger & always plenty to drink.
So be merry,
Who's throwing the party?
Does it matter? Only to you.
Peace come with us,
Guide us back to our roots.
Let the leaves be full of branches—Harmony!
Music always playing some kind of song,
To open the heart & feel some kind of home.

The Unknown Author

Let the eyes be opened to see the
beauty in everything created,
Majesty—God's presence
No death only peace,
How much more do we need? Nothing
Be thankful for what you received & in turn spend
it willingly.
Someone else needs it more than me.
Not saying I don't need it as well,
But it's too overwhelming for one to handle alone,
We thank you!

Sweet Delight

Four weeks of intrepid love,
Kiss the maiden who bares her fruit,
Yours to choose upon.
Talons stabbed in your back
Love is in the air
Take it in but beware,
No turning back
We just can't have none of that
Dance all night in sweet delight
Child of mine, child so blind
Open your eyes & see the light.
Tunnel vision better than none
Come on girl,
Let's have some fun.

Running midnight's race can't bear to see your face,
What a wicked child am I to dance in sweet delight.
Cut the cord lets go,
Free to roam valleys down below.

The Unknown Author

Such a pretty face
Don't really remember this place,
Something from long ago!
Familiarity, destiny is finally ours,
Come on now & roam with me
To a place where divinity is infinitely sweet
Yet only sweet to the grace of the heavens beholder
Touch it, take it in, you still can't recall
all the faces you have been.
Dream the dream of sweet delight,
Touch us all night!
Hold us all night!
Scream a little bit louder, baby!
Sing us your songs all night long,
Passage back don't remember where it's at,
Trapped forever in a place of peace & perfect
Infant being
What's all over me?
Something in my hair, covering me,
Dramatically swept away
Let's find a spot in the hay,
Horses be hungry now,
Let them go out to graze.
Enter into Heaven's home
Nothing left of living so,
Let me be,
Let me roam!

Time Flows

Time flows,
Bright lights glow
Under the evening skies.
Do you want to be left behind?
Left behind.
People there
Do beware
For the safety of
The Children.
The children of the aging sun,
What you did should never be done again!
Don't bother with apology
You sick demented clinical freak!
I told you I was crazy,
Was I lying or just behaving?
What gives you the right?
What gives you the right to judge me?
Time flows,
Bright lights glow,

The Unknown Author

Under the evening skies
Do you want to be left behind?
Because I'm leaving.
Off through the stars
Gone by far,
Try & catch me!
People with power use it wisely,
Your time will come, then you will join me
In the Heavens of the ancient Greeks,
All the Gods & myths are there watching the dreams!
Forgiveness is divine,
Forgiving what is alive.
You of the future be kind.
You know you hear it,
Let's listen one more time,
One more time
Time flows,
Bright lights glow,
Under the evening skies
The journey has begun,
We're there but not for long
(Love the Freedom,
Love your dreaming child!)

Help me be

Hello friend,
Nice to see you again.
I thought you were dead or just imaginary?
You look well,
May I go with you now?
I'm ready,
& willing to travel!
Teach me truth & wisdom
Help me be
I know you have up until now,
Make it real
More valuable,
Let it live & spread on the rest of us.
Magic energy,
Miracles
More than just dreams.
Healing the Sick
Curing disease!
Maybe even walk on water

The Unknown Author

Or fly to the top of the trees
Whatever it is,
Help me be
~Please~

The Focus of your Life

Children sleeping,
Women weeping
Alters filled,
Nobodies there!
What is the focus of your life?
Prayer
Petition to some savior,
Or thanks to a Creator?
Does it matter?
Do you care?
You're not even paying attention!
What's the matter?
Are you scared?
You forgot the focus in your life
Love in living—
Let me give you some insight
Thank you Creator for Life
That is the focal point,
The reason why we are here,

The Unknown Author

To enjoy who we are not hate it.
You are forgetting that God is always there
Realize that & move on with your life.
Evil is just a thought—
Think of something useful & new
Get all that other shit out of your mind
Then you find the focus in life
The focus in you.

His Victim

Confused as the mind maybe,
Desperation unfolds,
Taking its toll on
The killer's immortal soul.
Who deserves no better than what he has?
No one
The fool on the hill still weeps,
Bitter sorrow fills his heart,
It's tearing him apart.
What can he do?
The rose is withered,
The petals are almost gone.
There is no place to run
The path which once was bright is no more.
The killer has no sight
So he sits & waits for the day's light,
Which is sure to come as time passes on,
Just as it did before.
What was his crime one might ask?

The Unknown Author

It was hesitation that he grasped.
His victim, was himself
Which he killed with such pity that
even a blind man could see.
But no one bothered to look in his direction,
His victim was crushed by greed
Very disappointing wouldn't you agree?

The Key that mends

The gasp of darkness slowly fading,
The glimpse of light becoming clearer than before,
Hearts beating different now without rage,
Peace of mind?
I don't know
Hell is fading from you without pause,
You are happier now from what cause?
Soar like an eagle & touch the sky
Over trees & valleys you will fly,
Down foothills in the snow.
Swim with the whale as a lifelong friend
Peace be the key that mends.
I say again
Peace be the key that mends.
Nothing lasts forever,
Even the strong must go.
We are as one
In peace until the ends of eternity
My brother—My Friend

The Gift

I received a gift last night from a new born life,
This girl told me she loved me (My Future Wife).
My reply was thank you,
The connection was noticed as I gave insight to the future.
I told her I loved her as well,
& I do but more on a friendly level.
Because she is human, I didn't want to hurt her anymore
Than what was already bruised,
She's vulnerable & slightly confused.
I said whatever you love me for reminds you of you.
Maybe something you are looking for,
But you don't know what it is,
It blinds you
It is something you own.
We spoke of awakenings & how it will be
when all we need is each other in
A mystic place of eternity.
The gift she gave me last night
Was the key to Heaven's door

James R. Saner II

Energy flashed through my body—
Like I was invisible
Love, Kindness, Open hearts
Taking chances for something more.
We are all angels with many different messages
For many different people.
The connection is together
Already built steeple
We are the creation in the same big picture,
Why not come together & prove we are equal?
We do not want an end to the creation,
just want some answers.
The questions have been piled up for many years,
What is space & what is time in the real world?
The sleeping mind,
How many different levels to this life?
Innumerable measure, is the truest form of answer.
We all need some confidence
We all have answers,
Love the people & love nature.
The thing that makes the Creator angry is blinded people,
The ones who think they know everything,
Without wisdom you gain nothing.
Lower your guard, call off the defense,
We were put here as a puzzle with many pieces.
Let's come together
Together is the gift I love

The Unknown Author

Thank you for listening
God's will be done.
Peace go with you in the lifetimes to come—I love you all

What you face

A river flows upon your face
Here lies your simple beauty
To let me look upon in wonder.
To see such a side, a side of emotion,
A true side of what you feel & face.
But what you face is he,
He who knows nothing of your heart
& even less of your mind.
Can it be he makes you weep?
The rose he gave faded away & is gone,
Yet he still searches for your dawn.
He can't find it because your heart belongs to me,
Do I not hold its key?
What do you really face?
What is really wrong?
Can I help you or should I just go home?
Remember I love you & will see you tomorrow.

My Prayer

This is my prayer, Oh God
Creator of everything
Thank you for this life & Earth you've provided,
As you have shown me everything
My heart is happy,
In you I am grateful.
The energy that is present & I thought it was my own,
I realize it is only part of me as in
turn we all are a part of you.
No loving adult would ever turn their
back on children (Theirs or others)
You have many names,
So I will call you as Freedom.
One-way streets are OK,
I will wait for the appropriate time & place.
Thank you for believing in me & showing the way.
Sometime in the future or present,
Wherever we exist,
We will meet up & talk

James R. Saner II

Spirit to Spirit
No fear can enter the circle.
So I pray to thee, cast all my fears free so that I might gain
The Knowledge & Wisdom written in books.
Help me overcome so I might help others
& do what my soul purpose is.
Thank you for your time & I appreciate
the situations (Good or Bad)
That was a hard thing to say but I'm glad I said it.
All in good faith,
I will sing your song,
Thank you, Oh Great Freedom!

Grandpa's Dream

Grandpa's there in a dream
Healthy & gleaming
Dead to the world but alive to me
He is a part of everything.
He wiped the tears off my cheeks.

I watched as he tried to speak,
Too amazed was I to remember his speech.
So real was this,
I was surprised to see what was in his eyes,
So much love & a lot more life.
No pain or any grief,
He was young again & very happy,
My Grandpa no longer asleep.

He paid a visit to say hello
I love you & look what I have found—Peace.
He was living in another time & place,
With a swimming pool & a big staircase.

James R. Saner II

This mansion was beautiful,
The place where the pool was I can't explain.
The colors were clear & ancient.
So focused & correct
This place I wish I had never had left
I know I didn't,
This place is all around—Heaven
Make the best of it & don't lose it or
Take the chance of having to go through it again.
Spirits are watching & calling,
Not everyone is awake,
So wake them,
"It's not my call", he says.
That's ok, it has always been this way.
Choose the change,
The chance is all you have—choose it.
Will I see you again? Sure
Well then prove it.
I already did,
& that time if that is what you want
to call it is always constant.
Full of different ladders.
I asked him where my place is?
"You have to find it" was his last response
I think you have already found it.
For you it is the Red man's ways
Take your pipe & smoke in peace:

The Unknown Author

To the North, the South, the West, & the East,
Then lower it to the ground & give thanks
Raise it to the sky & offer everything!
Who you are,
Your presence,
Most of all your being,
Individual roll call if you will,
Partnership in trade & what you receive is nothing,
Which is everything in the same,
No greater than always equal,
The Spiritual way.
Walk through it,
You now have the key.
It's tough but you'll be OK, not everyone will agree
& that's how it has to be.
Hardship & sorrow are there,
A step to the clouds & beyond.
I love you,
I have to go now, I will always be with
you & I never really left.
I just want to say thank you to the spirits of now,
& to the spirit of my grandfather
who I love & admire dearly.
Always Love
(& now my Grandma has joined him & knows the Truth)
Become a part of that constant stream of Energy
Peace, Hope, & Love

Pilgrim

I am a pilgrim in this life,
I seek a smart & beautiful wife (She found me)
For love & peace to be mine own
& lots of land that I may roam.
My goals to be are simple
To live & be a part of nature.
God, I wish to please
& for the Spirit I called & then was answered,
Go to the Indians reservation.
I will help out my people so they may
See the Creator is still creating.
To be a child fee
& simply pray every day for peace.
A peace pipe to smoke with the elders
& a circle of trees will guide me.
I wish to seek a family of beings,
To be accepted by the spirits.
I give my life, it is no longer my own,
To God & to my wife who is soon to come.

The Unknown Author

Patient & waiting smoke inhaling,
I am cleansed by my actions. (Quit Smoking it is grouse)
Happy is my long lost task, living is all I need.
For the joy in life is in breathing & riding the wind.
It may all end & then I will be set free
Into the stream of energy
In everything.
So you see, I am a pilgrim indeed, we all are.

Tired & Alone

What you need
Is something you will receive.
Maybe not now but soon.
A Wife,
A Child,
Possibly a dog.
It doesn't really matter
Just as long as it's another.
Sick of being alone,
Tired of going nowhere.
To many people,
Too many ghosts & phantoms.
How lonely am I?
How lonely are you?
Has it even begun?
The dark bottomless pit
Of being alone.
Someone help us,
I know who I am, do you?

The Unknown Author

Possible figments of the imagination
But the question is whose?
The answer will come soon,
Eternity isn't that long,
Maybe just a few light years away.
No, I think the Who is here in this room
Writing & reading these ruins.
Me or just you…

Tuesday's Rain

Tuesday's rain has come,
The time of departure is gone.
Off to a world I will never call home.
They can't break me, my spirit will remain free,
No matter how high the wall, we shall overcome.
I feel the presence, oh, so strong
I'm by myself & all alone.
Is that as true as it may seem?
The Grandfathers are watching over me,
Making sure I don't crack & start the hesitation,
They already tried the medication.
My senses remained unharmed,
I will however go along & make them see that I am strong
Strong in body, mostly in heart,
Like the eagle who soars the skies looking for its prey,
I will be out of here someday.
I miss my woman & I miss my brothers,
Their presence around me is strong,
In my dreams they do come,

The Unknown Author

They come to comfort me & sing an ancient song.
To bring joy where the body & mind have none.
Fulfillment & then made happy
For the days are long in my penitentiary.
This is all I need to overcome & be made free—
The Brotherhood of the Three!
For all eternity

Hoped

He had hoped all was well,
She knew him better than anyone else.
Was that enough?
It most certainly was,
He had hoped one day to make her happy
& share his love for all eternity.
She had hoped this many years before,
Now she is with someone else.
He has hope for her safe arrival.
Is it enough?
One day we will find out.

Hope is everlasting,
Bonding the universe with Magic.
Loving Mystery

God's Confession

This is the legend
The spoken prophecy,
I shifted for experience
Mainly for escape.
I am aged beyond reason:
The Man, the Myth, the Spirit
We question because we care
Always about something.
I am God
Ashamed by my recollection.
I do not deserve to be what *I AM*
Who I Am
I created.
Everything you see is for me,
It comes for me
It leaves for me.
It seems no one will remember me.
I don't see good or bad,
I can't even hold my head up to breathe.

James R. Saner II

I wish you were God instead of me
Then I could believe in something,
I could have reason for my existence,
A purpose to be.
You my friend are lucky
The wise man's fantasy.
You at least have hope & the will to serve or create.
I do not tie my people down,
I let them wander in their curiosity.
This is my Father's house,
My Mother left him,
Their relationship didn't work out.
They both need to find happiness—Alone.
Then maybe share their Freedom with someone else.
Things happen!
Don't misinterpret my meaning,
For I am happy here
It's somewhat of a challenging environment,
I still need someone to teach me.
Is it too far off?
That God has a God &
His God he rules, too?
The latter of creation, the dream of evolution.
The writer who writes these words &
The ones who believe it
Know who I am & have come to peace in their heart.
Fulfill your wishes for the hope

The Unknown Author

Of a better future tomorrow.
Awaken at sunset
Fall asleep at dawn.
The night is a blessing, a peaceful meditation,
Time invariably moves with no questions.
Vampires, no
Druids, I suppose.
All who come to worship,
I take the blame for unanswered prayers,
I forgot who I was for the moment.
I am sorry for your losses,
The pain which brought you grief,
The Truth is you pulled yourself through.
Be ready to receive Heaven.
All who are awake & leading,
You must know the power is yours,
That which you have had from the beginning.
I am the present beholder of this Universe,
All that which is mine.
Yours I give it to you.
The mustard seed of faith
If you can believe
These writings will make you great,
Believe me when I tell you it is that simple.
Proclaim yourself to all that which is Holy & Righteous
Stand in the presence of the Almighty.
Your kingdom & riches will be given unto you.

James R. Saner II

You are the rightful heir to the throne.
Responsible for all life,
You must make sure it grows.
Share your freedom,
Share your love for me,
After all, we are equal.
I have just realized who I am.
Will I burn in Hell? NO!
To me the Truth speaks highly,
I can't and will not destroy anything.
As for death, it is the mystery behind life
Which makes growth possible to happen.
A valued ally
A true friend to life.
That feeling which you are receiving is almost like
You wrote these words to yourself.
Cherish this passage,
The rest is for you to complete.
Take a moment & look around,
Realize all that which is
Was given to you.
You should be proud.
Life has its problems
This is true,
Your role in life is almost through,
Lend your knowledge to another,
Share your compassion toward one another.

The Unknown Author

If you are enraged by my thoughts & dreams for this place
Then you have forgotten one thing—EVIL
You who hold grudges or envy another's traits
You of hate & convictions.
You are the Devil
With your foolish thought or self-doubt,
You make it so others can't
Find their way out.
You must end this negative thinking &
Realize that you are equal.
Show love & understanding,
Instead of judging,
Start listening & suggesting solutions
to this world's problems.
It is a great honor to be a part of this Book.
My Angels,
Your Angels are singing glory.
Let your soul receive happiness,
Let the children see,
Everyone,
I mean everyone you come into contact with
You must
Learn to treat them
Like Me.

The King

Conversation,
Meditation,
Philosophical explanation,
Everyone is forgiven.
Who thinks different or whatever is OK.
This is my own experience
My own opinion
From observation & contact with the great being.
Pointless words with so little feeling,
A true king reigns inside the heart,
It guides him.
The monarch of our times is you!
Treat your people well & listen to them.
Remember you are responsible to them.
This goes for every one of us to the
deepest part of who we are,
Which is the creation.
Do you believe in God?

The Unknown Author

Do you believe in Religion?
They are truly different things,
Still just definitions…

Messiah!

Messiah,
Messiah,
Why worship thee?
You abandoned your people,
Made them get down on their knees.
You promised them a second coming,
Where have you been?
Some king!
Where is your heart?
Don't you have any feeling?
You abuse your people & promise them eternity.
This doesn't sound like a God who brings peace!
Get me out of this Garden,
It's been great but too boring for me.
The funny thing about you Messiah is
I don't hate you,
This has to be miscommunication or fiction,

The Unknown Author

Where are we now anyway?
Are we real?
This part gets really confusing…

Remember

Why am I so afraid of leaving
Letting go,
Just disappearing?
Too scared to accept who I am & what I'm capable of.
Frightened when you realize the universe is really yours.
It's scary
When it's real.
God's gift (Words) mine & yours.
Come with me!
Share with me your story
I am listening.
Can you believe it, I created God,
In the same way he created me.
Partners,
Friends,
Freedom in the forest & the leaf caught in the wind!
Free to explore it,
The beginning,
The end!

The Unknown Author

I love life & cherish its secrets.
They are my own & I am theirs.
Why did I choose to forget?
The only answer I came up with is to
Remember.

Where does your Destiny lie?

Some people think your destiny is in your dreams,
Others think it's in your mind,
Trapped trying to come out.
I know where the destiny lies,
In dream land is where it cries.
Hoping for someone to come & take it away.
It prays there will be a way.
Billions of souls stranded,
Trying to find their way.
Looking & looking in the wrong direction.
Over here a voice cries,
I know where your destiny lies.
Come, I show you
I shall not lie.
Follow the one who makes destinies come alive.
Should you listen?
Or run for your life?

Back Together

Back together seems by far so undeserved,
But I ask you, can we get back together?
The one & true love in my life has called upon me
& it feels so right
But seems out of reach.
My heart strives to be one peace,
You are the part that is missing.
Let's get back together.
Our life together will be so free
& I will do everything in my power
To keep you protected,
No more pain or grief,
Just you & me forever.
You called for reasons far greater than your own,
The universe wants balance in love.
We are soul mates who have found each other.
Let's not lose it,
Let's just get close together & grow
in every possible measure.

James R. Saner II

Ever since the day we met I have felt you.
I have thought about you & remembered
the only time I have ever
Truly been happy & that was when we were together.
I am truly sorry for leaving before,
That has meaning unknown.
To be one together we must first experience separation,
Which we have done & now the year has come
It's time for destiny's measure.
I love you & ask you
Do you want to get back together?
I think it's a little overdue.
Fate brought you back in my arms
for a night to remember,
That is not all, unless that is what you wanted.
I imagined beaches longing to be laid on,
Children crying to be born.
It is a gift & I am thankful for every moment.
I might sound a little crazy,
But I really can't handle someone else kissing you.
It hurts in a certain place, & it's a
killer that grips the heart
Until it breaks & shatters.
I guess it's because we are supposed to be together.
So please give me an answer.
Let's get back together.
Yes, it was written in the Stars

Rose

A Rose is what lovers exchange when dating,
A flower that means something called love.
Love that is indescribable.
A feeling in one person's life
Trying to exchange with another.
But when the rose dies we weep,
For it was an exchange of one person's
feelings & emotions.
The love of the rose will never die in one person's heart,
That is something that lasts forever.
Even after you die
The rose is the only survivor.

Just as before

I'm all alone now,
Just as before
What a place this is to be,
No longer free.
What to expect, nothing
I started out here,
Left & came back again.
Hope someday to leave once more
& never to return
I thought differently about her,
She was my horizon,
She gave me peace then left me grief,
Just as before.
No longer am I loved,
No longer to be hugged,
Nothing here brings me joy,
Nothing here but little girls & boys.
I'm just a child now—alone
Just as before.

The Love of a Woman

The love of a woman
Touching you,
Makes your mouth water
As she kisses you.
She feels safe in his arms,
She's someplace she can call home.
Happy & pleasured they are together
No longer alone.
Total Heart Completion!
After love making they have soft conversation,
As they hold each other in one another's arms &
Dream of the future together.
He speaks of marriage,
Tears fill her eyes,
Are you proposing?
He says yes &
Waits for her response.
With a soft gentle kiss she said yes,
There is nothing more I'd rather do,

Then be your wife & marry you.
Good, he says
We'll make arrangements tomorrow.
In each other's arms they faded away
into the most peaceful sleep
Anyone could ever imagine.
They became one in the eyes of God,
Married, another seed was planted
Where it will bloom forever.

God Instead

If I were God
Instead of a man,
I would make some changes!
Only peace,
No more sorrow,
Forgiveness to all of man.
You all would be me & I you,
I mean you would be God too.
We would do it together.
Freedom—
Love for the Heavens & all of nature.
Energy brought us together,
& separated us for the experience.
Maybe for balance in your life?
Maybe for balance in the Universe?
This is possible &
Has already happened,
God is the great I Am.
Whose thoughts are these?

James R. Saner II

His is the truest answer.
He is the Creator,
The Alpha
& Omega
We are a part of Him.

TV

TV—Education:
Television
The life we live in
Sitcoms & movie channels
Who needs school when you got the
Cable Network?
Living our fantasies out through the stations
The Actors,
The Directors,
Billions of dollars collected
Biggest economic outbreak.
Let's do it!
Let's fly,
I think Star Wars is on channel 9
Who's got the controller?
He pushed the wrong button—oops!
Electrical shutdown all across the nation.
Read any good books lately?
Didn't think so.

James R. Saner II

Here's one it's called the Bible
But no,
You decided to call the cable guy.
He will be here in twenty minutes,
You have time to cook the TV dinners,
Then get situated in your TV watching position.

Visitor

To my own love am I true,
I leave your arms & I miss you.
Can I ever let you go?
I hope I never know.
Could you be the one I love for all times?
When I see you, my eyes become blind,
I only see you, you give me the strength
To conquer what's in front of me.
I feel your breath gently caressing me,
Everywhere I look
Everywhere I go seeking my desires,
Here you come to light fires.
You see my stack of wood & your eyes widen,
The pyromaniac found a bonfire.
Flames lit up the night skies
Jesus Christ arises
Passes go, collects his $200 dollars &
travels on toward Heaven,
Visitor.

James R. Saner II

Bodies covered in ash,
The lighting sent a flash made the
tree fall & orgasms happen.
The thunder roars with approval,
Sending rain to make the atmosphere more enjoyable.
Cleansed the environment & chilled the air.
The people disappeared through the
act of sexual movement.
Their energy level took them beyond
the outer reaches of Heaven,
Made them Angelic.

I'm seeing

Soaring like a hawk, I am happy.
Trusting what runs my life, I believe.
If I never live to see tomorrow
My spirit will then become free.
The steps of faith are tremendous,
They challenge me daily.
I am grateful for today & tomorrow.
Wherever it is I land that is home to me.
Wherever I go that is where I belong.
Judge me not, I live my life for you.
My brothers, all this is for you:
The mediums, the connections, the ones
who tell you, life gets better.
I have seen it, too. Buddha says hello,
Christ is on a cruise & wishes all of us well.
Muhammad is in his garden visiting
with his good friend Allah,
Who still says the joke's on you.
& for our good friend Lucifer

James R. Saner II

We give you thanks friend for the balance
needed to pull us through.
The angel who is on his way back home,
There is no need for any throne,
None was wanted.
The music, the beings, all life's creations is what I'm seeing.
We are ready for our arrival into open arms.
Glory be to everything
From the Heavens to my truest being.
I LOVE YOU

Observant Being

The drive,
Slow ongoing scenery passing through
the passenger's window
The Rockies,
Pike's Peak just out of reach,
The rich pretend it's theirs.
The tree line moves across the rock in waves
Aging mystery.
With millions of clues that lead you nowhere,
It's beautiful as it disappears.
Population moving in on old wilderness space,
As if they own it.
No one seems to care,
Who is truly aware?
The old grows old
The young grows with it.
We don't know what's out there,
We only know a little about what is here.
THE POWER,

James R. Saner II

The beauty of the mountains leaves me speechless.
So many colors,
The energy level here is enormous,
I feel the call of nature.
So I leave my company to find a silent spot—
The air is fresh & the fire is surrounded by a circle of logs.
Teepees symbolize my ancestor's presence,
As I sit alone with my thoughts.
The trees witness everything around me & bring comfort
Where there once was not.
My friend, the sun is setting—
The cycle of day is changing everything into *The Night*!
The change of season,
The growth of all life.
What is an hour to a day?
A day to a year?
Or a year to a lifetime?
What is a lifetime to eternity?
Where does it begin?
Where does it end?
Are you aware of it?
Sometimes;
It's OK to follow the blind,
The will get you there.
Even better, lead your own life,
Trust yourself,
Trust what has been provided,

The Unknown Author

Feel it move & guide you.
It's real & it will not lie to you.
Become the hummingbird—
Look & observe everything,
Take what is needed,
First we must find it.
I cannot experience another man's life or be like him.
Why would I even want to?
A simple reason is confusion,
Too scared to take responsibility for your own actions,
Your own thoughts & your own life.
Where one once was another will come.
They will be provided.
Not to take its place,
But to have its own feelings, thoughts, & life.
The one that once was has moved on & is experiencing
Their own way of life.
This goes for all creation:
The Trees,
The People,
The Rocks,
& All the Animals.
The Deserts,
The Oceans,
The Stars,
& So on!
Take a look at the BIGGER PICTURE,

James R. Saner II

Find your LIFE!
The wave of peace
~~~~~~~~~~~~~~~~~~~~~~~
The calm of the storm
~~~~~~~~~~~~~~~~~~~~~~~
I will not fight
****
I will only defend
****
In my pride,
I shine with honor
!!!!!!!!!!!!!!!!!!!!!!!!!!!!!
Through Heaven's gate I'm going
^^^^^^^^^^^^^^^^^^^^^^^^^^^^
Circles,
()()()()()()()()()
Triangles,
+++++++++++++++
Geometric Figures
##################
Space Time Continuum
<><><><><><><><><><><>

Definition

Everybody including myself would
like to know what God is,
This is my definition of the unknown:
He is great—
Loving, Caring,
Sharing, Thankful,
Intelligent,
Everything, Nothing,
Invisible,
Here,
You, Me,
The Mountains,
The Seas,
The Volcano,
The Beast of the Jungle,
The Monster of the Deep,
The Stars,
The Universe Itself,
Infinity,

James R. Saner II

Magical, Mysteries,
Lonely,
Happy, Free,
The Maker,
The Creator,
The Mirror,
The Shadows,
The Spirits,
The Devils,
The Angels,
The Christ child's,
The Children,
The True Experience deep down inside you,
Farther than you can see.
Ancient,
Truly Amazing, Religious,
Mental, Death,
Physical, Life,
Energy, Father,
Science, Mother,
Sons,
Daughters,
Conversations,
Belief.

I Love Them All

The storytellers,
The wish-it-would-happen-to-me people,
The ones who think everyone's going to Hell,
The ones who believe they will save your soul,
The non-believers,
The questioners & the seekers,
I wish you well,
I love them all.
I don't ask them to love me.
That is everyone's choice.
All I do is listen,
Then speak my peace.
This is all I will ever be,
Is this true or just fantasy?
SURE
Whichever is OK by me.
When people fall, they fall on me.
I give them everything,
My attention,

James R. Saner II

My being,
When they stand
They see me as just a dream.
Impossible, it couldn't be real.
Impossible to be known.
I'm just like God,
Abandoned.
I'm still forgiving,
Not self-pitying,
I am strong
Very loving.
Compassionate pretender.
I'm a giver,
Who speaks of truths,
No matter how unsettling they may be.
I share my peace
With the Universe,
With you,
Most definitely for me.
In my selfishness,
I bring you everything.

Upset Just a Little

No more nice things to say,
I betrayed my age,
Cut it off for some reason,
For which I can't explain,
All I know now is that it's gone.
My life must move on.
No erasing today's activities.
I betrayed myself,
Remorse is what's felt.
I turn my back on everything else.
I know no one will help get me where I'm going.
My hair can't blow in the wind, or be brushed out,
It's gone taken with it my
Identity & my heart.
Why am I so upset?
Who am I now anyway?
Do I just blend in with the rest of the flock?
I will NOT
My hair will grow back.

James R. Saner II

Wokini is the new term
Seeking a new vision,
A new Heaven.
I will not be denied,
Me is bigger than any ocean or any land.
God's vision is out there—
Whoever God is I would like to meet them &
Understand what it is I'm worshipping.
For the meantime
I worship nothing.
I believe in nothing.
I will become nothing.
I'm old & tired of playing games.
Have some respect for me shit,
All my writings & searching comes down to this,
You haven't made me happy,
You threw Freedom in my face & expected me to trust it!
Well, I failed.
I'm a loser,
I don't deserve to be here,
Neither do you!
Whatever that means,
I don't know, you figure it out,
You big pompous ass God.
Is there a correct answer?
What are you doing to me?
Can't you explain it a little better?

Control

Some things that you have faith in,
Always leave you hanging
On the side of a gravel road.
Dirt swarming around your face,
Perplexed by the atmospheric situation.
Journey we more my fellow man,
Journey we more into the future of us all.
Nervous energy awaits to be freed of boredom.
Taking steps little by big
To get to know who we are.
How confusing!
Possibly too much movement
No time of stop or rest,
Forever going one direction.
Is that it we have but one objective?
One choice in which to travel.
Control issues,
There are some,
But missing one ingredient—control!

You're out of control, use something else.
Find a new spring or fountain,
Find out how it happens.
Adults grow younger as the children age.
Two viewpoints,
We experience both.
We never grasp the phantoms.
Clean yet dirty, we have both always.
Minds wandering in thought or space.
Minds inside of minds times two to the infinite power.
Justifiable cause for escape.
Who's the captive & who's the prosecutor?
Whose court room?
Whose dream?
You come back to You over & over again!
I always come back to myself.
I am who I am as the writer & words to whom I
Write is to myself, my you, Am I, to the, you—me
Who?
Speaking terms,
Not quite solid trust & faith.
The foundation needs some work.
I can't even listen to myself anymore.
I hope I don't ignore him.
Me is not my purpose,
Me is taken care of by—
You are who I'm here for.

The Unknown Author

Please if these words touch you
Go with that,
Not the second wave of feeling that
makes you question the first.
Please free yourself.
Help me,
What in God's name is sanity?

Been Awhile

It's been awhile,
Since I've done this.
It's been awhile
Since I've spoken words.
It's been awhile
Since I've touched you.
It's been awhile
Since I've listened to you.
It's been awhile
Since I've be heard.
How well have you listened?
Too condemned by your own righteousness,
Forgotten purpose,
Passing judgment,
As I am doing now
Forgiveness,
I'm sorry.
It's been awhile
Since I've forgiven you.

The Unknown Author

It's been awhile
Since I've loved you.
It's been awhile
Since I've done this.
It's been awhile
Since I've spoken my confession—
As I am doing now,
Hiding nothing no more,
Seeking true righteousness,
From the heart,
My God,
The heart,
Love you I do.
The heart is my God,
The only thing that is true.

Chasing Heaven

Chasing Heaven,
The place
Or
The emotion?
Feeling so low sometimes,
Trying to reach for the skies,
Asking the questions:
Where
&
Why!
Thoughts of the mind,
Conscious wonders,
Subconscious answers,
Antichrist
Or
True follower?
The creators of Heaven:
Angels & Demons
Powerful energies,

The Unknown Author

Peaceful & then some are evil.
The balance,
The fence post,
Balancing act of devotion,
One side or the other choosing which is best.
Or sit there forever in protest,
Chasing Heaven.

True Story

The story of a Spirit,
A young man who travels & is aware of his experiences.
The goal of knowledge in hand
I play that role of the Spirit, & this is my experience.
Looking back on all that's occurred is difficult.
My first memory is when I was two,
Standing in my crib looking at my Angel
Beautiful entity who placed me here.
She told me,
I will look after you
Of course the room that I grew up in was blue,
The constant fear of sharks swimming in the carpet,
Flashing back in thought,
Realizing who knew what my life was destined to become.
I was such a compassionate kid,
I couldn't figure out why everyone
else was so shallow & rude.
I personally want to show love & affection,
Love of the Creator that floods through.

The Unknown Author

My heart was burdened at a young
age to be there for others
When they didn't think they could pull through.
I am still this way,
God was what I was raised with,
The fear of Hell engraved into my
memory or programmed
To make me struggle if you will.
Torn apart by feeling & knowledge of
a being known by man as God.
What a deal, my parents are younger than I am.
It's the truth of realization
Flooded sea of remembrance:
I've been a King,
I've been a slave,
Back in Egypt I set my people free.
I've been a Monk,
I've been a Priest,
I am an Indian born free—Native American.
Native to the land—Pandora—So many lifetimes &
History shares them with us.
I proclaim to know nothing,
Yet I seem to be learning everything—Vibration in feeling
Telepathy of the brain.
So many wars,
Based on religious greed,
Freedom is what we fight for now—supposedly

James R. Saner II

It to me looks like we're the schoolyard bully pushing
The little third world countries down.
To civilize & transform them into something
Americans can stand.
Warped philosophy,
Is that the kind of education we need?
Pardon me, my listeners
I apologize for looking so negatively
at our county's situation,
I bring a new solution,
Communication with each other.
Lend a hand to your friends & neighbors
Spread the wealth & you'll find your true treasures,
& we will lose our selfish selves
& gain the respect of our elders
& be able to look more into the future.
We have the opportunity to govern ourselves &
The right to see God's presence given new life.
Brothers & Sisters
I have found the new wealth
& health of the Spirit.
I ask you as just a man,
Less than equal to you,
Let's do this together.
The Earth already provides us with what we need,
Now is the time to prove ourselves worthy to nature.
I am but a speck of sand in this new movement.

The Unknown Author

The control is in partnership & expecting nothing.
We work all our lives in dull captivity,
Naturally we will need leaders,
I say to all of you who listen that
the leader we need is you.
If you allow your heart to breathe,
You will see how much you want to do.
It's not just my dream,
It's our dream.
Let us work to make this world more beautiful,
Let's only take & use what we need.
Finding happiness is a number one priority,
& helping others receive it as well.
Please, People
Please show yourselves,
We might die at the hands of those who don't understand,
Somewhere, sometime they too will know &
See what it is we died for.
When we grow in number
Is when we start marching on Congress &
The World
Let us build the New Kingdom of Heaven here on Earth.
We have the capability & chance to do it ourselves.
Let us stay out of the Heavenly Wars,
Let us small beings show them what true Independence is,
Even if it means my death,
I will not surrender

James R. Saner II

Our weapons are our hearts,
We will receive our enemy with open arms.
Cast away their demons,
Free them from their fears,
Show them who we are.
I ask for your support.
Our goal is not about winning,
It is about achieving knowledge
& the power behind that which is wisdom.
One man cannot change the world himself,
He has the right however to ask the
world to blossom out of its shell.

I

Party Habit

End of the day,
The start of night.
Activities that arise in the dark.

The night's dream,
Girls nude dancing,
Gets the mojo started.

Moving hormones imbedded in the drink,
A little love potion,
It gets the party hopping
There's a boy knocking boots in the back bedroom,
With a girl who's passed out.

Rat

I am the rat—
In somebody's experiment.
I am tested for I.Q.
Poisoned to see how much I can stand.
More than physically abused.
I am the rat—
In the scientist's maze,
I can find my way when cheese is displayed.
They move the walls to throw me off,
The cheese is what counts
My only objective—
I accomplished.
I am the rat—
Who escaped from my prison,
They made me a genius with one simple problem—
Freedom!
I figured it out,
Now it's time for the rat's revolution,
Specimens set up their own experiment!

Responsibility

The star collapsed,
Sending star dust on its way,
Mass floating in space,
Heading our way.
Human D-Day!
If impact occurs, who knows where you're going?
Probably be thrown out of your body,
Soul sent skyrocketing—
Across the Universe
A lonely eternity,
Eternity is yours,
How you view it is very important.
It is never ending,
Neither are you
So find emotion &
Use feeling to pull through.
You've read the same book
Over & Over,
Trying to see past the words,

James R. Saner II

Addicted to solving
Someone else's mystery,
It's time to create your own—
Responsibility.

Worlds Inside

Worlds
Inside of Worlds
Inside of Worlds
Inside Ourselves—
Some do look.
Different beliefs,
Different people,
Different situations,
Different thoughts—
Still constant movement.
The art of doing takes you forward
The direction which you wish to travel.
Learning every second
Of every minute
& every minute
Of every hour—Infinite knowledge
The mind wave of creation—The Solution
The man or woman who thinks they've figured it out
Limits themselves to nothing.

James R. Saner II

My advice—
Don't do this,
Smarter than that I imagine.
We will move forward,
Not taking life for granted.
Recognizing that we might not be here tomorrow.
Cherish this moment from now on as if it were your last,
Wisdom accomplished.

I See

I see
A man walking in the sandy deserts.
I see
A culture hurting—searching for a leader.
I see
A man approached by the serpent,
He rode it back to his people—Concurred evil
I see
A man walking in a forest
The native tribal leader.
I see
The spirits of this land gather around this man &
Show him signs of the future.
Visions—Invasions of different kinds of people.
America they shouted!
I see
A man sitting under a tree,
Meditating for inner-peace—Buddha
I see

James R. Saner II

A boy sitting under his tree,
With a wild imagination.
Writing & reading his books,
Divinity—The Holy One in his youthful age,
Referred to as God by most people.
I see
Me in his writings Life-long stories.
You were in it, I saw you there.

The Neglect of My Green

The neglect of my green,
So it seems I've damaged.
Lack of attention my green is lonely,
Please somebody come tend to it.
Lost sheep, maybe runt of the litter,
I've neglected my green too often.
Not the fault of mine—but the misfortune of others,
My green is tired.
Dying short of breath,
My green is gasping for a little respect.
The groundskeeper is 97,
Three years shy of 100
He's dead—my green followed.
Earth unkempt means,
Death for all on it.
I wept!
Never nurtured, but shortly forgotten,
The end has already happened.

My Fear

My Fear
I fear has trapped me here,
Scared stiff stuck to my chair.
Petrified—Silent screams,
Throat too dry for sound to escape.
Feelings of unexpected death stalking.
My Fear
I fear is taking over my brain,
Thoughts of zombies lurking.
Sign of delusion approaching,
My strength has left me,
Stranded—Helpless I wait.
My Fear
I fear is nothing more than a nightmare,
Just another crazy dream—searching for speculation.
No more pizza before I sleep—
Can't handle that pepperoni & cheese,
I had nothing that I can remember.
My Fear

The Unknown Author

I fear has left me here,
Lost & abandoned.
I am aging—dying as fast as I'm living.
My Fear got to me.

Torn & Betrayed

I keep my head raised.
I am not ashamed!
I was blind
But now I see,
Honesty is something we all need.
Feathers tied up
Mean people suck!
Freedom bell cracked
No longer ringing…

Trapped inside the Mind

Fortunes on this rainy night,
Tell me
That I have seen the light.
But I still don't know
Still can't find you
Still trapped inside
The mind.
Can you see me?
Can you lead me home?
Let's go.
Tonight we travel,
Tonight, Tomorrow,
Tomorrow I will be found
I'll meet you on the other side of now.
My love, My life,
The fortune teller was right,
The choice is mine
Do I surrender or do I fight?
I stand alone on this cold & rainy Night

James R. Saner II

Waiting for my praise to be answered.
But I still don't know,
Still can't find you,
Still trapped inside,
Your mind
Can you see me?
Can you hear what I am saying?
It's all right now,Freedom.

Hitchhiker

Driven down the road
Of endless thoughts,
Looking for a Hitchhiker to pick up.
Cars abandoned on the side of the road,
Left for dead by their owners.
The driver keeps on going.
Headed West toward the Pacific Ocean.
Planning on driving across
Next stop China.
Night goes by as quick as day,
One is really longer than the other.
The driver & the dog,
They take turns driving.
The dog has trouble reaching the pedals,
But manages to keep on moving.
The gas gauge reads empty
But still they continue through the streets of a small town,
100 miles east of the California border.
The engine shuts down,

James R. Saner II

They raise the hood
& put up a sign that states:
Out of order
Please drive around.
The Driver becomes the Hitchhiker
The dog stays behind with the vehicle—
Abandoned…

The Day of the Magic Sun

The day of the magic sun comes only once
Every ten thousand years.
This is the time—
Expect it.
The children see & do believe in
the history that is present.
Ancient ones who shared their message
& passed on its brilliance
Will be there.
The dead will walk & the living will be still.
All heads will be lifted.
This day of the sun has some strange message
to share with us as the listeners.
All things will become one & the
pressures will be nonexistent.
The peace we all have been waiting for is now given.
The day of the magic sun will be remembered & respected.
The next one is the last one
So cherish it,

James R. Saner II

Don't you dare miss it!
Not intrusion,
But willingly look upon another
If they allow themselves to look at you—
& see you for who & what you really are.
Then understand what you view
& how it can be that simple & possible.
I wish it was something someone could tell you,
But it is not.
It's something that
Comes from you—yourself.
Has to be equal.
Distributed fairly
So as not to offend or
Invade on someone's private space.
We all have been in this type of situation
I can tell you it sucks.
Terrible feelings felt.
Worthless—Unsettled.
Growth will happen
No matter what.
As it gets easier
It gets harder & vice versa
As it gets harder
It gets easier.
Impossible but
Possible if tried.

The Unknown Author

Explored, Observed,
Yet still here,
Our world must really love us,
Or just doesn't care.
Missing my comfortable self—Forgotten
We are still sleeping.
Freedom on a jukebox,
Freedom in the Mind.
The feeling of Freedom
Remembered & Cherished
For the time mentioned.
Somehow still forgotten,
Eternal plea of devotion.
The writing was laid out
Ready to be read by
Someone who will read it.
Mine I suppose, sure go ahead,
The thought of intriguing curiosity.
Upside down to me,
Facing the interest in Mind.
They overlooked
What was already overlooked.
They left.
Just another nobody,
Just another word missed—Misinterpreted!
A Blues Traveler,

James R. Saner II

Going with that soul he puts in his pocket.
Music the voice of strangers.
Truth to the performers.

Train 109

Last call—
Train 109 leaving,
All aboard!
Soul Train just left the station,
You missed it.
"Damn it!"
Late again as usual!
"Oh well,
I'll catch the next one."
"When is it?"
Not tile tomorrow.
"What time?"
Evening noon
"Not till midnight,
What am I supposed to do?"
Catch it!
Same thing I told you last time,

James R. Saner II

You have to come sooner.
"Or what I'll miss it?"
Good conclusion…

A New Song

The stress of life
& slowly dying
Fading away
Into the nothingness
Of forever
Dreaming the long days away with work & dedication
To family & client
Who needs me now?
& now that I am ready
We may begin
To end up here
With great reward & accomplishment
I can sleep now the end has arrived
The night has grasped on to my body
& then I awake with light through my window
Born again anew into this ever waking moment
The song has not yet been sung
The dance is taking shape with each passing movement
As I stand now with a sense of purpose

James R. Saner II

I find again that I am the same man I
Was before
Not just a man
But a spirit of now
The ever dreaming
Sharing being
I have the answer you look for
Is it in the questions that we ask?
Or the ones we don't
If you take one person & teach them the secret
Then maybe you may have your rest you so want
But if that one person doesn't share it
Then you have to start all over
Again
&
Again
Searching for more space
The right face
Place to be
Or leave
I'm not going
This way that way
Maze of the unknown
Game of chance
I miss the romance
The chase of more…
For I have been asleep

The Unknown Author

& now I am awake
I seek once again the answer I so searched for
Is it in the one we find ourselves?
Lost inside somewhere
Could it be that simple?
One being
Recognition of the spirit
Does the name mean anything?
Temple of the most high
I sing praise to you
A little song
Not so long
Just a simple thank you
Thank you
Simple in the difficult situations
Very hard to do
Master of the obvious
I thought maybe this was so…
For just a second I thought I was normal
Then the most amazing thing happened
I found out I am not
For I have been given many gifts & many talents
Anointed by the most high to bring peace
to those I come into contact with
Every person
Young or old
Every living being

James R. Saner II

I feel with my heart
I share the peace I know without words
By how I present myself
For you can see in me the things you desire
& you can be with me your most sacred self
For I have seen with my eyes the spirit work
Through us,
We are the body
From the head to the toes
We are the answer to the problem
Let it be so that I bring the blessings
Given to me by the creator
& let it be so that I then bless you
For in my blessings of you
I am blessed more.
A smile is simple
& yet so hard
We struggle in the day to day
& end up lost
I say find me
For I am not far
I am, wanting to be found
Use me as you see fit
For I will be but for a moment longer in this time
& then I will be gone
Left behind are the memories of another
For I am ever becoming

The Unknown Author

Growing beyond this passage…
Into the next & so on
Could be better or worse
Who knows?
Out in the field
Someplace up on a hill
Side really,
Waiting for you to come home
& meet with me,
Bless me & take away my sorrow
Spread the seeds of tomorrow
No more pain,
I need healing in this place
Eternal
I brought with me
My own body
Original source of origin
I have come now again into this garden
To give back my sins
For I no longer need them.
But for a moment the ghost stopped
& whispers in my ear
Sorry all souls are final
Sold into slavery
By my way of living
Going & going
Trying to not rest but yet

James R. Saner II

It is so hard not to stop,
The spinning of the wheel
The great mystery becomes far more
& then the darkness
On the edge of light
It suffocates me
Freedom inside this mind
I tried to find an escape, but I'm still here…
Forever
Once again at this pace
I move on
Along who there is beside me,
Nobody home
All alone gone she's not happy any more
Doors open wide
The windows closed
Days awake & the nights too dark
Round here somewhere
I saw the ball role,
Flip of a switch
Just a twitch
North Pole to South Pole
Bi polar,
Train wreck happening
Before my eyes
I can do nothing to stop it,
Choice of the spirit

The Unknown Author

Function
Act now
Or get back
For the motion is constant & the balance is none
Forget about the so called normal
Or the option for rest
Always something to take care of
Something to fix
I didn't even know that it was broken
My heart can only take so much,
Stress the key to a short life
Just let me hear you bitch.
Nothing is good enough
No better than worst
Sick is not to healthy
Emotional turmoil
Roller coaster ride
Not to highI'm getting older....
Adult life,
Fancy party
The constructors of the city,
Have another drink lets
Pat ourselves on the back
Good job
Just to do it again & again
Today is tomorrow as
Tomorrow is yesterday,

James R. Saner II

So on &
So forth
I flunked the course
I thought for a moment that it
Was about money & growth,
NOPE
Debt & taxes
All work & no play
Ice skates & dance
Doctors & bills
Medicine bottles empty
Last pill fell down the drain &
The plumber's late.
Cocktail dress
I made a mess
All over my good pants
Just another one
Shoot it up good
Don't remember a thing
Must have been one hell of a party,
Show case
Ballroom
Last award of the evening
Ladies & gentlemen
May I present to you
The king & queen of sorts
Not even a standing applause

The Unknown Author

Who cares anyway, lets
Go home....
Attention everyone
Attention,
Yes now thank you,
Are we having a good time?
Learning as we go,
Do you think you could stop?
As I say go,
Moving on in this place
I saw a face
& then it was gone,
A drift on the clouds
A sense of wow
I could touch the sky
& hold the moon
Put as many stars up as I want to
Freedom
Worth every dime
Blood flows & rightly so
Ramble on man
Gamble on those numbers
By rite of passage I
Calculate
& they are man's number
Can it be?
That we have

James R. Saner II

Made a mistake
YES
NO
Always & forever
Motion in the universe
Answer in the question
I confess
I know not
To look & see
Something
That is or isn't there
Doesn't really matter
The before & after…
A knock at the door
A please & thank you
Welcome
A message
This is a wise investment,
A testament
Preach the good news
Share love & a blessing
I give these to you
& I bless your home
If you see who I am then you bless me too
Just a lonely saint
On my way in this journey
Up that damn hill

The Unknown Author

& back down again
Struggle is a tool
I get the picture
I share my whiteness
I am forgiveness
As I am forgiven
May the walls fall down
& bring you into the new days light
Out of the mother's womb
& away from the tomb
A life lived forever
My soul
& my temple
By morning
I have forgotten the night
A new day begins
& on to the next
Instant
Or moment
Do you have the time? I think you do…
Safe in this place
Many in the one
Trying to regroup & be that again
Just for another instant
I want to go back
& do what I didn't do
I want to change what has happened

James R. Saner II

Not really no
I like my mess & I feel myself
Can we grow any better than?
Before the time could not be traced
So we just were
But now we track the movement of the Earth
How it spins & so on & so forth
When the mass
Takes shape & has structure
Continuing to move & maintain motion
On some sort of course or direction,
Not just moving randomly throughout the cosmos
We see the battle of light & darkness
It is scaled out to the very atom
We are a part of something so much greater
We can't even see it,
Too big & yet we really are that small
Funny really
Self-importance is
On course to complete
What already has happened?
Today is tomorrow
As tomorrow is yesterday
So it's true we already have been.
& so we will be for a long
Long time…
Now take this very time

The Unknown Author

& remember
Or regroup
Come back to yourself
For a moment
To think we live but once
& then it's over
Just begun
Plain as day
Night settles in
Blanket of depth
The walls fall down
The game just now over
Win or lose
I gave it my best shot
To have it all taken away
Just in a second
Now it's all over
What happened to this life?
This dream I had of growing up
I think I feel older
I see my children
Just keep growing up
Beautiful
To catch our breath
& be filled with the spirit
Second wind to keep on going
I will see you at the gates

James R. Saner II

& walk with you to the other side
Just not right now
Work to be done
& ideas to be shared
Have a seat in an empty chair
& now we begin to expand our horizons
& lead like we're supposed too…
Welcome to the TOP….

Must be allowed entrance
To this most sacred place
Space of sanctuary
Room to be shared,
A collection of the body
Holy cross of spirit & blood
Brothers & sisters
Sons & daughters,
The love that bonds &
The love that makes
All things possible
All things pure,
Music fills the place of loneliness
A new song is sung
we move on to prepare a place
Come forth king of kings
Welcome back to this plane
Your absence has been

The Unknown Author

A Hardship on so many
Let your healing wash away the pain,
Walk with us spirit
Baptized & cleansed in the most high
Name above all names!!!
Praise beyond our understanding
Comfort in our shortcomings
Faith in our rock
The word of yours in our hearts,
Take refuge in this heart this
Temple of ours
Let your spirit have safe passage
What is mine is yours
I thank you for the gifts
I take accountability for them
I will grow them in your blessing & send
forth your spirit into the world
I am
The way & the Truth
I have the grace from above
It is my gift of salvation
That I give to thee
For I do not deserve any such blessings
The level of understanding
Be with me
In struggle I will prevail based on strength
Beyond this body

James R. Saner II

I will not give in
I will fight to the ends of eternity
I will protect this heaven from he that
Wishes to take it
Thanks be to the creator
I pledge myself forever
Amen!!!
A healing wave of passion
Walking around me
The forerunners have been chosen
They will bring your love to the world
The world will seek your love
As have I
& as I am found so to
Will the lost be lifted up?
We are yours & we sing your song
Through the day & through the night
Until your day comes & you have
A thrown upon the earth to sit upon
Thank you for the gifts
Of music
Of writing
Of speaking
Of singing
Of healing
Of being
Thank you for so many…

The Unknown Author

Be free from this choice of choosing!!!
Has not the mountain been raised
from the depths of the sea?
So too will the spirit be raised from the earth
& given a new body to dwell in
Dance my people
For the coming of the son
He is soon to come
Again into the realm
A new time has begun
A new dawn
So to a new love
Love of life
Love of peace & light
A journey of collective souls
Beginning again in the hearts of men
Awaken in the presence of ours
Be filled with the spirit
So that the spirit will become once again
Alive & wholesome
Let there be balance in the heavens
Let the markets be free trade
Help us reach your poor,
You're hungry
You're lost
Help us find them all
Give us the lessons to teach

Give us the wisdom to lead.
Thank you father from above
My most high love…
I do not know what is to come
But I will be here to face them
I will watch for your coming
& I will work for your spirit
I am forgiven
I am forgiven
My sins are gone…
I will greet this day a new & with open
arms. Thank you for this new life!!!
Thank you for this new song
Days away Good Friday has come
The Lamb was taken,
The journey begun,
Place me not in this instance
Places we have been
Traces of a past life
Lived or forgotten
Glory is the Fathers
Faith through the Son
Death fulfilled and life concurred.
Split hairs counted and combed
You knew me before I was ever born.
Do you remember breathing?
The first time screaming,

The Unknown Author

War cry to the beings,
Presence known…
Cast away the shadows,
Bring the light into the soul
Heaven has been waiting
Let's go…
Just for a moment the time stood still
We gathered our thoughts to make it
Until completion was still,
We are who we choose to be
The perfect creation growing in a dream
Catch the next train moving
Tracks only go one way
Passing through the movie
Life projections filmed
Mirrors only show reflections
Hands lost in the vision
Mind trapped in the maze
Let me sleep now,
Waking dreams
Theatre closed until
Someone brings me the keys,
& so I wait
Fiddling with the lock
There must be another way…
Without choice there is no Freedom only slavery,
Without pain there is only bleak moments on a scale

James R. Saner II

Unbalanced, no understanding of healing.
Order in motion one single line
Can be twisted and crossed over many times,
Without death there is no life, just a simple kind of Existence,
Matters in time and motions come alive to break
This mold that has been created, shaping a new Day
Taking with it the rest of this one's future,
When the past is lost or forgotten it is reborn
In this present reality as something of a New Age
Of Knowing, trying to understand is impossible...

NEED

(Money & Food)

I.   Long time coming pen to paper
Dream to reality, shift in time courage to maintain the course
Trails left for others to follow

          Elements that seem to be against you
The winds they seem to shift without reason
Always blowing some direction.

II.   Pieces scattered minds
Worlds' collide spinning wheels of destination
Sunrises, Time lies in waiting

          Constant motion, oh to be still
Patience…

III.   Forward thinking this insanity away Grey between
        The Black & White lacings
        Moon & Sun Dancing

        One radiating & the other reflecting
        Illuminating the image of Light
        Casting its shadows

IV.   Manmade clouds
        What happened to the real ones?
        Patterns in the sky grid locked
        Universe & Truth racing chasing the tails of time
        The fabric of the future passed off as Today
        Which really is yesterday made into tomorrow

V.   The signs they are all over written for the journey
        & follower
        Circles & numbers the common wonders to get here
        Climate control to Hot but oh so Cold
        The Wind does blow

        A light in the dark
        Faces traces of a not so distant Beginning
        Ending in mystery,
        How amazingly interesting

VI. Being trapped in silence
 Taking shape with every (Sound)
 Glorious music vibration of
 Life forcing greatness to
 Happen
 Action
 Forward motion
 An ocean to explore above & bellow

VII. Bodies inside the spirit
 Spirit inside the bodies
 Adhesives bonding the universes
 Holding it all together giving it form
 A part of not really separate

VIII. Ciaos in order
 Stream flows down hill
 Light hovers over the trees
 Glowing, space just on the
 Other side of the blue border
 Dripping white milk shooting
 Stars symbols formation
 Exact placement, falling away
 From or moving toward

IX. Living is Dreaming only
 Awake instead of sleeping

Vessel filled with water
The cup runs over Destiny
Meets fate late for the tea party
Sugars one lump or two
Sweetness can be uplifting
Burning Energy, Consuming
Substance, what is left wasted

X. Beauty of Creation pondering the wonders of Heaven,
Greatness in the elements
A being of always
Realizing itself without a mirror
There is no reflection
Without another there is no us
Only empty space
Whether it is light or dark
Still alone, a whole lot of nothing
Something

XI. Rock of ages
Plains of existence flying around
Vessels inside vessels
Blood flows,

Heartbeat
Voice screams

Wounds bleed

Fuel that feeds fire
Tune the radio frequency
Currency exchanged
Trades begin
Growth Domestic Products

XII.   Hate of self all alone
Manic in a state of euphoric bliss
Then the bottom falls out
Line drawn on a graph trying to stabilize

Sensations
Depression
In a moment can be
Uplifting

Realization of the Creation
Mystery closest to the
Truth of our existence
Reason for Being

XIII. Rectify the senses
Give shape to the plan
A collection of designs
Modifications to perfection

Execution of the actions
Needed in doing,
Trying hard to remain constant

Success brings failure sometimes
However winning is by far
Better than losing
Either will be obtained by choosing.

XIV. A child leaves the nest
Only to return as an adult
Bringing equity to its parents,
Trained to hunt & survive
Sharing its kill

Value to the tribe
Leadership in the community
Life cycle

Family is most important
Blood lines
Flow the course of centuries
Thousands of Histories
Personal & collective bodies
Only a few recorded
Even less shared or remembered
Organization

The Unknown Author

        So much bigger than originally thought as being
        Patterns through time
        Treasure map
        Secrets

XV.   River flows where it flows
        Nothing will completely stop it
        Path of least resistance

        Creative destructive force
        Self, serving
        Life source

        Marking the lands it moves over
        Divided banks are how
        Bridges are formed

        The Earth is ever consuming
        Burying the living,
        Once dead
        Dust just as before

        There is no escaping the cycle
        To live means dying
        Or being reborn

XVI. Leading means following
Fighting for what is right
Living for something more

Understanding greatness at its core
Value is established in a Collective Body
Recognized as the best currency
To move ever forward

Chasing the Sun around the Earth,
Dancing with the stars
In whichever present cycle of Completion

Guessing the outcomes
Which team is winning?

Last chance to vote

XVII. Laws of nature
Fit for survival
Strong preying on the weak

All going to die,
Finite in the borders of this spinning body
Infinite on the inside.
Truth as a breeze blows
From nowhere

But somewhere it goes

To breathe comes
From effort
Work it takes

Blood flows from the Heart
Drum beat
Life source
Only reason for Life
Pump it up
Slow to fast

Solid
Liquid
Gas
Science of reason
Assumptions

XVIII. Closed eyes
Seen is music
Painted on a canvas

Reflections of memories
Some past
Others haven't happened
Future potential

Sick with want
Taking care of needs,

Overwhelming Life
Is a disease
Chronic fatal condition,
Maybe just a dream

XIX.   Remembrance of the past
Cycle of beginnings
Just as today brings endings,

Structure of order
Is collective consciousness
Humanism established

Body of works & experiences
Race to break free from
Formalities

Shift in realities
Advancement in understanding
Constant growth of being
Maybe Becoming

XX.   Religion,
Collective practice of Principals

To influence the civil order
In Mind, Body, & Spirit

To establish growth together
& individually

Politics, the division of order
But the balance needed to rule

XXI. Sight, Sound, Smell, Touch, & Taste
Senses of nature
Connecting the body

Centered is the mind
Collaboration of parts
Creating a whole

Always with motion
Once direction is aimed
& ignition fired

The object is launched
Into space

Only thing that stops it
Is impact

XXII.   Everything in season
For a reason
We begin, understanding

Comes in the form of
Projection & Recognition
That we are limitless

& will continue on for the Ages
Purpose established for the benefit of others

Fruit grown & harvested to nourish
The young ones
So they may grow into awareness

XXIII.   Connecting the dots
Casting lots
Waking into this body,
Lines on a graph
Points in between
The gleam of light & its reflections

XXIV.   Angelic language
Whispered into existence
Forgotten language
& reborn into this generation

The fallen cry out to the Creator
Forgiveness

What once was Lost
Waste & recycled
Fuel that feeds the fire

Burn brightly
The light of the World

XXV.   Projections of futures past
&& we are told to believe,
But never taught how too

Spirit is the Truth
Of what we are &
What we exist in

XXVI.   Powerful healing beings,
But for a moment
We thought we were alone

& then we see far beyond
The self

Growth & judgment
If we realize that all is

As it should be

Then we will
Have Joy in our Hearts

XXVII. Resurrection in a new day
Dawn rising
Inspiration
Uplifting presence
Fullness,
Imaginary walls crumble
Openness,
Vulnerable spirit
Healing,
Outreach songs being played
Prayers being heard

XXVIII. Corporation
Growing platform
Loud voice,
Past is done

Now is happening
& what is to come

Future knowing
Praise room 24 hours 7 days a week

Outside & Inside
Worlds collide

XXIX. Burning man
Running out of too much time
Is it safe or sacrificed?
Offering, Give a little and give a lot,
Nothing can be something sometimes
The quiet is still too loud a silence
All alone but not lonely
Build the alter
Across our dreams
Show me where it leads,

On the path
Less traveled shall I be
Come with me

XXX. To the Earth
I go ashes fall like snow,
Cycles

Up & down
Still spinning around
As a clown paints tears on his face
The body holds real ones in place
To thirsty to let fall

XXXI.   Death is in us all,
        Ghost lingering

        Glue that binds us
        Denied is self,

        Leaders rarely follow
        & followers rarely lead
        Connecting everything
        Spiritually

        How long until we are here
        In Eternity

XXXII. It is with aging
        That we grow into wisdom,
        Spaces
        Emptiness
        Void or lacking

XXXIII. In essence, Substance
        Fill the emptiness with kindness
        The loneliness with peace
        & everything else release Joy

        For it is truly
        Overflowing reflections of the

The Unknown Author

        One true being
        Whose image we are

XXXIV. Angelic tongues
        Silent languages

        Chanted & released in dreams
        Powerful healing voice

        Presence scabs the knees
        & leaves imprints on the forehead

        If not for compassion
        Then what?

        To exist solely as a higher form
        Of self

        Invisible to the lesser realms
        Whispering ancient secrets
        To the few who were chosen

XXXV. Something must be given
        In order to receive

        How to be space for belonging,
        Hearts filled up with every kind of
        Emotion,

So many to choose from
Which one is the closest?

Motion
Like the revolutions of the Sun

Fast is perception
The measurement of time,

Some hearts beat faster than others
& some slow themselves down

XXXVI. We must get out of the way
Of our own destiny,

Recognize that it is farther reaching
What is believed to be seen

Center folding in on itself
Multiple happenings & simultaneous
Possibilities

Reactions of awaking from a dream
Or reality once thought of or
Imagined as impossible

Accepting your Creator as Holy

&filled with goodness,

Love for itself
Portrait
Love for its You & Me

XXXVII. Christ's greatness comes from
The suffering of our human condition

The fact that he took it all on himself,
Passion that all would be accounted for
& all would be saved

Encompassing all would be well
Depth of understanding
Comes only by way of acknowledgement
That we are limited only by perception
& universal laws

Time,
Gravity,
Fuel,
& Temperature

Perfect balance is
In order

Made in the USA
Columbia, SC
28 February 2025

a5dbc251-0d35-42ee-b695-173da7def247R02